ETERNALLY ROSE

By LOU MASTANTUONO

Based on a true story

As told to Mary E. Davis

This book is a work of creative nonfiction based on a true story. All events and opinions were portrayed and represented to the best of the author's recollection. While stories and scenes in this book were based on actual events, situations, and incidents, they are shared from the author's memory and suppositions. Some names and identifying details and locales have been changed to protect the privacy of the persons involved. No parts should be taken as medical advice or scientific fact. The author has attempted to share a story aligned with actual events pertaining to the narrative herein. This story is intended for entertainment and is not intended to offer opinions, defame, cause harm, or malign any person or entity.

All inquiries may be directed to Covert Operations, Ltd at acovert@covertop.com

Photos courtesy of New York Daily News and LIFE Magazine.

Paperback ISBN: 979-8-9859756-1-1
Digital ISBN: 979-8-9859756-8-0

First printing April 2022

DEDICATION

In loving memory of my dear mother, Lena V. Mastantuono, who was the pillar in my life, as well as in the lives of many others in my family.

"Just get it done" – Promises made, promises kept

"Morta! Morta! Morta!" a middle-aged Italian woman cried out on that warm Sunday afternoon.

Men and women craned their necks to try and get a better view amid all the chaos and panic. People flooded from the church doors and stood, shocked and crying, on the lawn outside. Men held sobbing women in their arms and offered cloth handkerchiefs to dry their tears. Several people fell to their knees, unable to comprehend what was happening, but also unable to move as they absorbed what they'd witnessed. Small prayer circles formed as townspeople desperately prayed together and asked for a miracle.

A young woman approached on the sidewalk, shocked by the unfolding scene. She stopped to take in all the hysteria and pandemonium. Voices wailed as the distraught crowd mushroomed in front of the church. Cars slowed, some stopped, and others had drivers who'd parked and run toward the church to see if they could help. Bedlam erupted as the crowd grew and shrieks, cries, and gasps escalated. The young woman paused on the sidewalk. She wondered if she should walk toward the mayhem to try and help. Instead, she decided to run to a nearby house.

"May I use your phone?" she urgently asked as soon as the front door had opened. "There's an emergency at the church, I think!"

Then, without hesitation, the kindly homeowner swung her door wide open. She stepped back and waved the woman toward a nearby black telephone and gestured to go ahead and make the call.

"Operator, an ambulance, please! We need an ambulance right away at Our Lady of Good Counsel," the woman said as she impatiently shifted. "No, ma'am, I don't know any more; I'm sorry. But people are screaming about someone being dead! Please, send someone quickly!"

CHAPTER 1

"How did you feel about everything once you'd learned about all of it? I've only heard parts of the story," my girlfriend told my mom one afternoon in the spring of 2000. I held my breath, afraid to meet my mother's gaze. We didn't talk about it often, but the ghosts from it still hung in Ma's house, silent and lingering, but long since put away.

Instead of being surprised by the questions from Debbie, Ma seemed almost at ease with the topic, maybe since so many years had passed and so much had happened. I knew she'd always considered Debbie to be like family, and that, since she presumed Debbie and I would one day end up married, Ma would be okay with talking with her.

"That's a question that's hard for me to answer," I heard Ma reply. "For a long time, I wasn't entirely sure how I felt about it, and the story is very complicated. But no one promises us that life will be simple, I suppose."

Debbie settled into Ma's brown floral sofa and pulled an embroidered throw pillow onto her lap. I'd long known that my girlfriend had wanted details about the strange story. For years, it had blanketed my family like an opaque veil, only giving an obscured glimpse of the truths that came to be. Oddly, my mother had always seemed at ease with her place in the story. Yet I had often wondered what she had sacrificed over the years.

"I'll go and get us some drinks from the kitchen," I offered. It would be a long afternoon, and I'd heard it all before. I already knew Ma's story, and I was glad she liked Debbie enough to share it with her.

Our home was like most of the other ones on the block. Privacy was at times something of a premium in our house. Most Italian families were like that, though—close-knit and in each other's business, as if everyone under one roof were a singular unit, operating in tandem and sharing the same vision. It was one of the things we all loved about our neighborhood. Being surrounded by families like ours felt comfortable. Everyone worked hard, cared about each other, and did their parts to make life easier for the next generation that came after them.

Even when a disagreement broke out between the families or among neighbors, it was rarely anything that couldn't be resolved over the dinner table while sharing a meal. When I was a young kid, I wondered if Ma put something special in her gravy, some sprinkle of magic that made everything okay again, since everyone was in a better mood around the dinner table. As I got older, I realized that it wasn't Ma's secret ingredients at all. It was that Italian families had long ago built traditions around their dinner tables, the heart of the home where they gathered. When people broke bread together, they found a common ground that always brought them back together, as if sharing the same food somehow allowed them to see one another's points and consider different opinions. While this worked in our house, too, I couldn't help but always feel that there was a little something that remained lacking and unaddressed, like people didn't dare get too close for fear of what could happen. The dynamic was sometimes confusing. As I grew up, I always imagined my family to be a gigantic puzzle—with one piece perpetually missing. I'd always felt a need to find that elusive piece that would satiate some unseen hunger for answers.

As a boy, I had sensed it. As a teen, I had seen it. As an adult, I felt it. Was it because I had changed or because others did? Had I matured and learned to view life and my family differently through the eyes of an adult? For decades, Ma had seemed to wrap herself in a passive acceptance. It had been that way for as long as I could remember. She wore that acceptance like a protective cloak, always crowned with a permanently set smile that hid so much.

When I was a boy, my heart hurt for Ma whenever Dad was insensitive to her. But that iron cloak of hers seemed to be all she'd ever needed, her suit of armor against his words and his dismissive attitude toward the woman who fiercely loved us all. I'd never understood it—any of it. I had wanted to be like the other families on our block, but we were different, and I'd always sensed it. At least, I had always *felt* that we were different. But try as I might, for many years, I never could figure out why. I never could peel back the opaque veil that prevented me from seeing the whole picture of whatever it was Ma hadn't wanted to share for so long. I thought I'd never find the hidden puzzle piece that would make me complete and provide me answers.

"That's not even your *real mom*!" the boys had teased one evening when Ma had come outside to call me home for dinner. When I'd turned to run toward my mom, I flipped off the boys with my hand behind my back as I raised my Wilson baseball glove to let Ma know I'd heard her. I'd listened to similar rumblings before. I had always ignored them and shrugged off the taunts as some half-baked nonsense.

*

"Frank, bring Debbie some pignoli cookies and some of that mustazolli, too," Ma said as I handed an iced tea glass to Debbie.

6

"I made the mosto cotto juice and the mustazolli myself," Ma added as she turned her attention back to her captive audience of one seated on the patterned chenille sofa. "The mosto cotto juice is important. I do it just like my mother taught me. Just use a bit of the burnt ash from the woody parts of the grapevines to cook down the juice. Gives it a richer flavor. Some say it's the rich taste of the earth in it that keeps us close to our family roots. I'm not sure, but my family has done it this way for generations—and Frank likes it that way. I hope you'll let me show you how to do it one day, Debbie."

Ma was always so hospitable to everyone. She liked to sit and visit and swap stories. It was probably a relief to her to be able to talk with someone, especially someone with a genuine interest in hearing the details of what had felt like my family's most taboo secret. We never talked about it. No one had said not to discuss it, but we all somehow knew to steer clear of it, lest someone open Pandora's box of secrets.

"Just let it be, Frank. Leave it alone. It was all such a long time ago." That had always been Ma's answer to me: just leave it alone. But I couldn't do that for the longest time. Years earlier, whenever I'd tried to press her for more, Ma had decisively shut me down.

"We're not dredging up past ghosts, Frank. There's no use in it. It's over. Let the past just stay in the past and look forward. We can't change the past."

I'd always somehow innately known not to talk to my dad about it, the forbidden subject. And it wasn't that my dad had told me not to speak of it. He hadn't. In fact, Dad never told me much of anything. He was a man who kept to himself, one of those men who felt it was his role to be the stalwart backbone of our family, the fortified port in any storm.

But I'd wondered about so many things over the years, so many tidbits of incomplete details that had only led to more questions. So finally, in time, I'd had to learn to make peace with the likelihood that I'd never know any more about *it*, about that mysterious, one-syllable *something* that had overshadowed my family's very existence.

I never brought it up to my dad. I had always instinctively known not to bring it up with him. It was because Ma had once abruptly changed the subject when my dad came home from work one day. My mom's raised eyebrows and pursed lips—cast in my direction, but only after Dad was out of eyeshot—had padlocked the discussion once again. Yet I was sure that I'd never get anything beyond "Let it alone. It doesn't matter today. That's old news."

Eventually, I learned to move on and not to nag Ma with my inquisitive nature. Plus, let's be honest, by the time I had discovered girls, my priorities had changed, and it was easier to let it go and focus on more pressing things—like a date for Friday night.

When I'd told Debbie the little bits of the story I knew,

she'd become just as intrigued as I had once been. "Yeah, well, if you get any more outta Ma, you must be some kinda mind guru," I'd told her. "Believe me. I've tried, and I only know so much, even today."

"But your mom may feel like talking now since some time has passed. Women confide things more easily to other women," Debbie had joked.

Debbie had been my girl in high school, years earlier. When we graduated, her father had insisted she go off to some university in South Orange, New Jersey. I'd heard their family's story enough times that I could recite it verbatim. "Our family's lineage goes back to the Setons," her dad repeatedly told me. "Debbie's mother and I could not go to college, but our Debbie must go. She has a responsibility to the family, to Elizabeth Ann Bayley Seton and all the work she did in the name of education and religion—but mostly religion—and our Debbie is a good girl with the same values as the original Setons."

Debbie never bought her father's story. "Dad, how can we be related to the Setons if the Setons were a Scottish noble family?" she once asked.

I had wondered the same, since all the Italians I knew had last names ending in vowels. But Debbie's dad didn't skip a beat when he launched into his trademark puffery. I could recite this part of his monologue, too, but I always stayed quiet and acted interested, out of respect, like I'd always been taught. I still silently recited the words in my head as Debbie's dad said them.

"My daughter, I have explained all that to you," he told Debbie as I listened one day. "Our family joined with the Seton family in the late 1700s when a Seton bought a violin from a Felipe Felicci in Leghorn, Italy, and the two men introduced their adult children to one another."

Now, Debbie had always been the curious sort, and she wanted more answers. So, she went to the local library one day and researched what she could. She never had the nerve to tell her dad that her research had found that a *Filippo Filicchi* had been the one to bring the first Stradivarius violin to the States. "He'd never admit he's wrong," Debbie laughed. "Besides, he'd just say that the original spelling of our surname was changed when our Italian ancestors came over on the boat, and the immigration people weren't been able to deal with all the vowels that we Italians use. It's one of those things better left alone, I guess. What's the point, right? What's it hurt?"

In that case, I decided that she was right. No harm was being done if her dad believed his family was connected to the Setons. That story somehow had comforted Debbie's mother and filled her with ancestral pride. But Debbie's parents weren't thrilled when she ultimately opted to go to beauty school instead of the university.

It had been Debbie's dream to open her own salon one

day, so it was no surprise that when she went to beauty school our relationship took a back seat. To be honest, we were both young, and I had a bit of a wandering eye, so it was inevitable that we broke up and began dating other people. I would see her every so often around the neighborhood, and although we were no longer an item, the flame never died.

I placed the tray of cookies on the coffee table in front of Ma and Debbie. "The dresses were just gorgeous, like straight outta the bridal fashion magazines," Ma continued, just as I'd heard before. Neither woman blinked as Debbie remained transfixed on my mother's recollections. But, of course, I'd already heard plenty about the bridesmaids and their gowns, and, if I'm being honest, that part of the story had never interested me too much.

"I'm goin' out to the porch for some air," I said, although no one acknowledged or even glanced at me. Instead of paying me any notice, my mom was thrilled to be able to talk about *it* with Debbie, maybe since some time had passed.

Like a slow-pressure cooker, poor Ma had held it all inside for so long. As she spoke, it was like watching that pressure cooker as it started to rattle and steam, threatening to blow the lid off the pot and into the ceiling as more and more parts of the story escaped her.

I was grateful that my mom and dad had always liked Debbie. I remember Ma rejoicing when I had told her that Debbie and I were dating once again.

"She's such a good girl, Frank. I heard her father talk about that story of the famous violin for so long, I was surprised when she didn't want to go to the university where her family had been."

I didn't bother to explain that Debbie and I had always thought her dad had given life to that story all on his own. I just nodded and left it alone since I'd learned to pick my battles over the years. Some things didn't matter as much as others.

Ma's voice trailed off as I stepped out to our front porch. I could occasionally hear just a word or two when Ma was dramatically recounting an impactful part of the story. But I didn't hear a peep from Debbie as she absorbed every syllable that escaped Ma's mouth. I knew, even without looking at her face, that Debbie was mesmerized by Ma's memory of that fateful day, the day that had changed everything for everyone.

CHAPTER 2

As I relaxed on my mother's favorite rocker on the front porch, a soft breeze made Ma's heavy wind chimes sway and ring. I still remembered when Dad had bought the hanging wind chime for Ma. I'd been maybe eight years old, and my parents and I had gone to Grossman Farms in Malverne, a small neighboring town a few minutes away. My parents would occasionally shop there for seasonal fruits and vegetables. This time Dad had bought me a hot apple tart, so the day stands out in my memory. He'd carried the shopping bags for my mom that day. His simple gesture had stood out to me because I had always wanted Dad to be kinder to my mom, the woman who'd always put her family first, even if it meant putting herself last. Ma had looked so happy on that day at the market when my dad bought the gold and white wind chime for her.

"Oh, it's beautiful, John!" Ma had gushed. Only she called my dad by that name. He was Johnny to everyone else, but he was John to my mom.

For years, I never understood why Ma had looked crestfallen when he'd shown her the wind chimes he'd bought for her. "The sounds reminded me of church bells," Dad told her.

When we returned home that day, I asked Ma if she wanted to go out and hang her new wind chime. She hadn't wanted anything more to do with them.

"Oh, you can go ahead and find a nice place for it," she'd said.

I couldn't understand how she'd gone from being so light and happy to looking sad and lonely. It had seemed bizarre that Ma now avoided the wind chimes, as if they no longer held any importance to her, after Dad said they'd sounded to him like church bells.

As the old story unfolded inside Ma's living room, I watched the large metal chimes sway and clang in the gentle breeze. I took in a deep breath of fresh air and thought about everything. It really bothered me that my dad had felt the need to be so thoughtless to Ma at times in years past.

She was such a good woman, not just to me but also to my dad. Ma had the patience of a saint. She'd always been pretty in my eyes. But then, I suppose all boys think that about their mothers, the first woman they love and the woman who's ultimately the measuring stick, for better or for worse, for all the women to come.

I had watched for most of my life how Ma had painstakingly taken care of our home, cooked our meals, kept our lives organized, and loved and protected us fiercely. Ma was the foundation of our family, the steadfast, dependable rock who offered support to everyone else. She was the glue that had held our family together for decades and the consummate wife and mother. Ma made it her life's mission to take care of her family. Our house was always spotless. Ma was a fantastic cook. She was the perfect hostess. She'd been a good and decent person for her whole life. And Ma could stretch a dollar like nobody's business. She was creative and innovative, and she even sewed her own curtains and sofa covers. Ma's fingerprints were on every part of our home. (Well, I guess not *every* part. But I'll get to all that.)

As awesome as Ma was, Dad didn't seem to notice her, not for a very long time. As a boy, it had seemed to me that no matter what she did, Ma seemed virtually invisible to him. I'd never understood it, but maybe that was why I'd always gone out of my way to be extra kind and complimentary to my mom, as if I could somehow make up for what Dad didn't give her. I wanted to see my mom's genuine smile, not that sad, empty, dejected look that sometimes crossed her face before she could conceal it. Even as a boy, I made it my business to know if Ma got a new dress or if she'd gone to the beauty parlor. If Dad wouldn't acknowledge her, then it would fall to me, my parents' only son, to lift her up and keep that smile on her face.

I'd always had a special place in my heart for Ma, not just like most sons do for their moms. This was different, more profound, and more protective, as if I'd had to look out for Ma and keep any hurt from getting close to her. She was a strong, proud Italian American woman. For years, I knew she'd always held something inside, as if she'd been afraid to let it escape into the atmosphere. I wondered how long a person could hang onto a secret or a pain until they could no longer bear their burden.

For most of my life, I hadn't known all the details of how it had all come to be. Yet as I grew older and matured, I watched my parents through different eyes. They were those traditional parents, the ones with age-old values, good work ethics, and pure hearts. They were proud working people whose greatest joy was their family and the knowledge they'd provided for them and raised them right.

Mama DeFabrizio and Papa Vito were also good people, right down to their cores. They were the neighborhood parents who were revered and respected, if not wholly feared, by everyone's kids. But it was the same for plenty of my friends' parents, too. Italians, especially Italian mothers, seem almost interchangeable when you're a kid. Step out of line or let a curse word slip in any Italian home, and the mother in that home instantly morphs into *your* mother when she flings a wooden spoon in your direction. Being respectful, especially to one's elders, was as important as breathing back then.

Just ask my cousin Carmine about the day Mama D deftly flung a baseball-sized meatball at him, hitting him squarely on the side of his bulbous head. A reminder that Italian mothers hear all. But, in all fairness, Mama D had a good read on us. Carmine and I had played Little League baseball together and gone to school together, and since Mama D had watched us grow up over the years, she was at the top of the pecking order in our neighborhood.

On the day of the meatball incident, we had gone over to Mama D's house to pick up her grandson, Richie, to play ball when she overheard Carmine talking about how a girl in our class filled out her sweater. We heard the swoosh of the spiced meat as it flew from Mama D's hand. Even before it hit him, Carmine flinched and ducked—but not soon enough. Mama D wielded meats and kitchen utensils like juggling balls and samurai swords. Rumor had it that she'd once tossed spinning pizza dough into the air and then hurled a rolling pin at her son—before catching the dough again— without even looking in his direction. Mama D didn't miss a beat, and she heard all.

As he rubbed his head from the smack of the cold meatball, Carmine and I didn't dare say another word. He slinked down in the kitchen chair and looked sideways at me with wide eyes. I kept quiet.

Mama D added, "You *respect* a girl before you can'a love her! No forget that! You full'a prunes, you boys these days! Now, go get'a some ice on that, Carmine, and have a piece of stromboli while you think about that'a mouth of yours."

Carmine and I silently ate the stromboli as Mama D walked outside. "You're lucky she wasn't in here a minute earlier to hear what *you'd* said. You'd be dead!" Carmine snickered.

"Nah, Mama D loves me like she loves my dad." I grinned as I took another bite of what would be my second lunch that day. Dad only took me over to Mama D's occasionally, just when I was young; and it was always by myself, never when Ma was with us. As I got older, he didn't take me as often, though.

When we went to Mama D's, her kitchen always looked like she'd been cooking for weeks. A delicious aroma filled the air, and it was always a given that one would eat at Mama's D's. No one could turn down an invitation to eat his fill at her table, and this pleased Mama D to no end.

"No touch'a cake," she sometimes said. "It's for a neighbor retirement a'party." Or she might remind us, "Eat'a broken cookies and leave'a good ones for me to take down'a to church."

Over the years, I figured out something about Italian

mothers. Once women become mothers, they apparently learn that food must accompany everything in life—every milestone and every moment. Food plays a part in all events. Birthdays, communions, holidays, funerals, and every weekday ending in a *y* must involve food, delicious, homemade food. Italian mothers believe food can fix anything from a broken heart to a broken skull. And given how well as Italian mothers cook, it's hard to disagree. Mama D's homemade pizzas were better than any we'd had at the best pizzerias. My dad told me he'd been eating her pizzas since long before I even came along.

For most of my life, I'd presumed Mama D to be a blood relation in my family. She was just like family, and she'd always treated my dad like her own son. For as long as I could remember, my father and Mama D had a special bond. He even called her Mom, but I knew that couldn't be possible since Dad had another mom, my grandmother, Maria. But as much as they loved each other, it had seemed like my dad and Mama D shared an underlying sadness, some unspoken pain that neither spoke of anymore. It was almost visible, like a thin gray veil draped over Dad and Mama D. As a kid, I ignored it, but as I grew older, I wondered about how Mama D and my dad knew each other. But, of course, I wondered about lots of other things, too.

*

Mesmerized now by the dancing, cross-shaped wind chimes, I

sat down and thought about how everything had come together over the years. There were lots of moving parts to the story of how it had all gone down and affected so many lives around Inwood.

I knew with certainty that Ma and Debbie would be planted in Ma's living room for a long while. I repositioned myself in one of the big chairs on the front porch and shut my eyes to reflect on all that Debbie was learning about inside.

It had been my Aunt Gina who'd finally put the pieces together for me, but only because I'd left her no other choice. And even then, I'd done some digging and filled in the gaps. For years, the story had predicated how my family lived and behaved, the way our relationships had formed, and even how futures would play out for many people.

Feeling a sense of calmness, I leaned back in my chair. Suddenly, I heard a nearby window open from the inside. Shockingly, Ma had moved from her captive audience to open the window for some air. I could hear her voice more clearly now.

"So, I was walkin' home from my job at Grant's Department Store in Far Rockaway where I was an office manager, and it was the oddest thing. It happened so suddenly!" Ma told Debbie. "Like out of nowhere, there was all this hysteria and activity! So many people and panic—like someone had disturbed an ant colony and sent them all scurrying. The church doors flew open, and people—there were so many people all over the place, all at once! Someone at the church screamed, 'Morta! Morta! Morta!' and I froze for a minute, afraid to move. I mean, if someone was dead, what could be happening? Right? I mean, could I be next? You just never know, even back then. So, anyhow, I was finally able to move again, and for a second, I thought about running toward the growing crowd, up ahead near the church. Neighbors came outside and stared up the street as small groups gathered on lawns and traffic stopped as drivers tried to figure out what had happened. Everyone looked worried, although most weren't even sure why. Women covered their mouths and gasped as they pulled their small children closer and watched and waited."

"That's crazy! So, did you go to the church? Did you walk down to see what had happened?" Debbie asked Ma. "Who was it that had died, anyway?"

"Well, now hang on," Ma told her. "I'll get to that."

I knew Ma was pacing herself. Since she could finally talk about it, Ma liked the crescendo moment as the story bubbled out to her new audience. She'd held it all inside for so long that I didn't begrudge her the gradual unveiling of the details. It was the least she deserved.

"No, I didn't go down there into all the madness," Ma went on. "And at the time, I didn't know who'd died. But word travels fast around here, you know."

Ma took a long, pregnant pause. I knew she was allowing the impact to settle in on Debbie so that she could fully take in what would come next. That was another thing about Italians. They're great storytellers who have a deep connection to their family's histories and traditions.

Ma started talking again inside. "I knew Our Lady of Good Counsel was s'posed to have several weddings—six, I think—on that day. So, since it had been an unusually hot day, I figured that maybe a guest had had a heart attack, or someone had passed out from the heat. You know, somethin' simple that had maybe gone bad quickly. These things happen, right?"

"But it wasn't that? I mean, it was none of those things?" Debbie asked.

I settled into my chair even deeper. It would be a longer day than I'd thought. Ma liked to ease into the story and then drop the clincher. But, like I said, it was the least she deserved, and probably a relief, to be able to finally tell the tale of what had happened so long ago.

Ma's voice and the lazy, melodic tinkling wind chimes relaxed me to sleep in no time. It was a good thing, too, because I knew that when Ma finally finished regaling Debbie with the big *it* of our family's history, I'd need enough energy to keep up with Debbie's endless conversation. I knew Debbie would need time to process all that I had come to know about the story. She and I had a good bit of history between us, too, but our story was nothing like Mom and Dad's, not even close.

I'd asked Ma countless questions myself and had developed a mental movie reel of how the story must have come together. I had played back different parts of the story for many years as I digested the secrets they'd all kept for so long. In a town where everyone knew everyone else's business, I was amazed that the truth had been kept buried for such a long time.

Johnny, my dad, grew up with that hometown good-boy reputation, the one that parents loved, but peers, not so much. Johnny seemed to have it all. Charisma, personality, good looks, goals for his future—all of it. He'd always been a good-looking boy, and as he grew into a man, people always said Johnny looked like Kirk Douglas, right down to the chiseled face and signature chin dimple. But Johnny wasn't full of himself. Well, not when it came to his looks, anyway.

As a kid, Johnny learned that he could make some extra money playing pool. He wasn't just good. Johnny was *great* at playing pool. And the fewer people who knew it, the better for young Johnny.

**

"Hey, what about that guy, the one smokin' out there?" Johnny's buddy Vinny Napoli asked him one afternoon as they walked up to the Walcott Athletic Club, where they'd regularly play pool.

23

"Yeah, good call. He's new around here," Johnny agreed as he and Vinny walked past the guy and through the open door of the pool hall.

When they walked into the dimly lit, smoke-filled hall, Johnny walked over to his favorite table, the one that locals left open in case Johnny came in. He waved hello and held up two fingers to the owner, who would regularly tend bar. Vinny and Johnny weren't old enough to drink, but Alfredo was a close family friend, so he'd always let him slide. Uncle Al, as they called him, always enjoyed watching Johnny's smooth salesmanship blend with his skills with a pool cue.

With the eight ball centered in the rack, Vinny racked the balls and aligned the apex with the center of the far end of the table.

"You wanna break?" he asked Johnny.

"Nah. Go ahead," Johnny said as he opened a pack of cigarettes.

"Hey, you want winner?" Vinny asked the stranger who had just walked inside. "It won't take me long to whip this guy's ass, trust me."

"Sure." He nodded. "I'm just gonna grab a quick beer first."

The stranger walked over to the bar and ordered. Then he turned around and leaned on the bar top to watch Vinny and Johnny, clueless that the boys had played out this exact scene too many times to count. The regulars knew Johnny. Most had known him since birth, and they'd always enjoyed watching his prowess as he ran the table.

Vinny made a few shots, but Johnny sunk even fewer balls. Finally, after a while, Johnny sent the eight ball down the length of the table and into a corner pocket—but there were four of his striped balls still on the table.

"You lose, buddy! Don't worry; I'll work with ya!" Vinny said as he slapped Johnny on the back.

The stranger from the bar came over. "Okay, so I've got the winner?" he asked.

Vinny put up his hand. "Well, to be honest, I need another beer. How about you play with this guy and teach him a thing or two?" Vinny said as he nodded toward Johnny.

"Yeah, whatever," the stranger agreed. Johnny let the stranger break. "Solids," the guy said after a solid ball jumped into a nearby pocket. Vinny held a straight face as he watched Johnny fail to sink most of his striped balls. In no time, the stranger had won. "Another game?" he asked Johnny.

"Guess I need the practice. Sure." Johnny laughed.

"Let's make it interesting," the man said. "Two bucks?"

Johnny acted reluctant but agreed. He shook the stranger's hand firmly to seal the deal.

Uncle Al and Vinny exchanged smiles as they knowingly watched.

"Aye, guys. A beer?" Kevin McCarthy nodded to Uncle Al as he walked up. Kevin sat down sideways on a barstool so he could be amused as he watched Johnny pull off his next hustle.

The stranger made a few shots, but Johnny deftly sank ball after ball. When he finally missed a pocket, Vinny winked to Uncle Al and laughed. "He's just bein' a good sport."

"Just'a make a'sure he no a'take him for all'a his money. I a'want him to spend'a some of his a'money at the bar, capisce?" said Uncle Al.

The stranger made his next shot, but he missed the one after it. Johnny coolly pretended to size up the table. Finally, he leaned down, lined up his cue, and with a cigarette between his lips, he sent the white ball fast and hard to the end of the table. *CRACK!* Then he did it again and again and again, as the stranger stood speechless and wide-eyed. *CRACK! THWACK! CRACK!* Johnny didn't look up as he kept his focus on the work at hand. With only the eight ball left, Johnny stopped and took a drag off his cigarette as he eyed the table.

"Eight ball, corner pocket," he called.

Johnny then turned his hip to the table and aimed his cue from behind his back. The stranger knew he'd been had. *CRACK!* The eight ball slammed into the corner pocket.

The stranger pulled out a crisp two-dollar bill from his pocket and slammed it onto the table. "Son, you are a hustler," he said.

"I've been called worse," Johnny laughed. "Double or

nothin'?"

But the angry man just walked out of the pool hall as Vinny walked over and smacked Johnny on the back. They'd run the same hustle since the ninth grade, and each time was better than the last. All the locals knew Johnny. Even Kevin McCarthy enjoyed watching him run the tables whenever a stranger came in. But Kevin was most interested in Gina, Johnny's sister, and had been for some time.

Johnny always concentrated hard on his pool game unless Rose came in, since he couldn't focus on much else in her presence. Of course, when you saw one, the other was usually there, too. But whenever Rose walked into a room, everyone felt the shift as Johnny stopped to look at his love. Friends and family alike knew they'd get married, and most were happy for them. This was because the guys wished they *were* Johnny, and the girls wished they were *with* Johnny. He had been the cause of many a high school girls' sleepless nights. It was the same for Rose. Beautiful, articulate, and intelligent, Rose was quite the catch. A grade ahead of Johnny, she was one of the most popular girls in school and the gem that every parent hoped their son would find.

Johnny and Rose made the perfect couple. Everyone said so. He was the handsome jock and she the smart, pretty girl who had always held his heart. Their bond was so storybook that Johnny's friends often razzed him about it. Rose's girlfriends envied her. They clamored around her on Monday mornings for a debriefing about Rose's weekends with Johnny. "What? No! Tell us about it again," a friend of Rose's squealed. "Tell us that part again about what his dark, wavy hair felt like in your fingers!"

"No! Just get to the important stuff, and tell us what happened next!" another girl protested as she swatted her friend. "Rose, get to his lips. Tell us what his lips felt like—all of it, and leave nothing out!"

The guys never got as many details out of Johnny. Rose's boyfriend was a gentleman, not the kiss-and-tell type, like most teenage boys. He protected Rose's reputation, and he cared about her as if she were a piece of fine bone china, too delicate and perfect to chip or break. If he'd touched her alabaster skin or run his large hands through her wavy hair, he kept those memories to himself. Their relationship was more important to him than locker room talk with the boys, and he intended to keep it private and hoped to make Rose his wife.

While Johnny only had eyes for Rose, he knew some of the other guys would love to move in on his girl. But he also knew Rose, and she only had eyes for him. But during high school, Johnny announced his plans to enlist, and the news was met with mixed emotions. Some worried about him going off to war. Others were glad to see the popular jock leave town.

"Don't get any ideas," Johnny told a couple of friends.

"Don't try and move in on Rose while I'm away. I'm comin' back, and you don't wanna have me to have to deal with, I promise you that."

Finally, his friends raised their palms in defeat. "No way," one said. "We hear ya, pal." But Johnny still wasn't sure about a couple of them. He knew there were a few guys who'd had their eyes on Rose.

"What'a about a'your high school diploma?" Johnny's mom had asked him.

"I'll get my GED later. But right now, this is what I have to do." His father was proud of the strong young man he had raised. His mother worried she might not see her son again. It was a scene that played out in countless American homes, and people stayed glued to their radios for news of the war.

Inwood is a hamlet located on the south shore of Nassau County, on Long Island in New York. It was a quiet area, far removed from the bustle of New York City. Most families lived in modest single-family houses, and people waved to neighbors during their evening walks. Everyone knew their neighbors—and most knew everyone's business, too. That's because news traveled fast in our neighborhood, which was made up of too many relatives and cousins to count. If anyone wanted the latest gossip, they needed only to visit the kitchen of an Italian mother. She made it her business to know what went on with others, especially if they had anything to do with her kids or family.

Most people were hard-working and family oriented. Life was simpler back then, in the forties. There were no computers, no cell phones, no video games or TVs for that matter—none of the distractions of today's world. In some ways, life was just easier because people knew their neighbors and had more time to be involved in the lives of others. Neighbors with gardens shared their vegetables, and women always made extra sauce on Sundays to share with whoever might stop by. Johnny and Rose wanted to buy a house and fill it with children one day, so they could raise their kids as their parents had raised them.

Since their families had come over from Italy, they all had their eyes on the prize. It was the American Dream, and everyone wanted their piece of it at the time. Most were patriotic and felt they had to do their part for their country to earn their right to it. Johnny was that way, too.

"I've got to go," Johnny had told Celia, his tearful sister. "But I'll be back."

"No, Johnny. I don't want you to go. You can't leave me," Celia pleaded.

Older than Johnny, Celia was born mentally challenged. So, she'd always seemed to Johnny like his younger sister and someone who would never get past the intellectual age of a young schoolgirl. This was never a negative thing in their household, and Celia had never seemed a burden to their family. Quite the contrary, everyone had always adored Celia and her innocence. She had always looked at the world through eyes that saw only the good in people. Just like an innocent child who had never seen the horror of man, Celia trusted everyone and never expected she could be taken advantage of or hurt. Her family always protected her and looked out for her, and while Celia loved everyone she met, no one compared to her brother Johnny.

"You can't leave me, Johnny," Celia cried as Johnny tried to talk to her and reassure her.

"Tell you what," he said. "How about if you hold onto my baseball cards until I get back? Can you take care of them until I'm back?"

Celia's eyes lit up as a smile spread across her face. "Your baseball cards? All the cards, even the most important ones you said no one can touch?" she asked.

Johnny hesitated and internally grimaced at the thought of jellied hands on his prized cards, but if it made Celia happy, he'd allow it. "Yep, all of 'em. But don't handle them too often, okay?" he laughed.

"Got it!" Celia squealed as she flew into Johnny and hugged him tightly. "It'll be my job to keep your collection safe until you get back, Johnny!" She grinned.

Johnny looked like a Hollywood star in his perfectly fitted army uniform. But with his movie-star good looks, he already looked the part of an American hero before he'd even shipped out.

"Just come back to me," Rose said for the hundredth time as she wrapped her arms around his neck and hugged him tightly.

"You just wait for me," he whispered in her ear. "I'll be back."

He hadn't told anyone, but Johnny was nervous about leaving his beloved Rose. She'd always been faithful to him, all throughout high school, but Johnny couldn't help but feel anxious knowing the vultures would be circling waiting for him to ship out. Everyone knew that as an Italian American soldier, Johnny would be considered a minority and would therefore go to the front lines before other guys.

But that didn't matter because on that fateful December 7, at the Walcott Athletic Club where Johnny had been shooting a game of eight ball, his mind was instantly made up, without pause and with no hesitation. Uncle Al had turned up his transistor radio as news of the attack on Pearl Harbor sent shockwaves throughout the club. Heavy silence fell over the bar as everyone drew nearer to the radio on the bar top to listen. Johnny knew that there was nothing he could do but serve his country and do his part. He had been raised to work hard, do the right thing, and stand up for what was just. There was a camaraderie and a deep, visceral patriotism that burned in the veins of most young men at that time—Johnny was no exception. *Not* going to fight for his country wasn't an option.

Several months would pass before Johnny was old enough to enlist, so when the day finally arrived for him to leave for boot camp, he was anxious to serve.

"You'll always be *my* hero, Johnny," Rose said, with tears in her eyes as she kissed him one last time before he left.

"No! Johnny is *my* hero!" Celia said as she tried to wriggle between the kissing couple.

Rose and Johnny laughed as they sandwiched Celia and hugged her between them. Johnny had always loved how Rose treated Celia like her sister. He knew that one day, when their parents were gone, Celia might have to live with him and Rose. But he also knew, even without asking, that Rose would be okay with it since she loved Celia as he did. It was just one more thing for him to adore about the girl who'd one day be his wife.

A taxicab pulled up to the curb as Johnny's family stood together, some smiling, a few in tears.

"Write to me, okay?" Johnny said to Rose as he hugged her just a little longer.

"Every day," she said through her tears. Johnny inhaled the scent of Rose's shiny hair one more time and then forced himself to let her go.

"Be careful!" "We love you, son!" voices called as Johnny handed his suitcase to the cab driver, who tossed it into the car's trunk. Celia and Rose clung to one another and forced smiles as they watched the cab until it was out of sight.

CHAPTER 3

Johnny's first letter arrived to Rose. "Mama! *Mama!* Johnny wrote back already!" Rose's hands trembled so badly that she couldn't hold the letter still enough to read it.

"You want me to read it, Rosa?" Mama D laughed as she took a hot loaf of panettone from the oven.

"Yeah, here!" Rose said anxiously. But as Mama D took the letter, Rose jerked it back. "No! No! Wait! You can't read it, Mama. It might be private!"

Mama D laughed and started to turn back to her bread.

"Wait, Mama! I'm still shaking too much! Stand in front of me and hold my wrists steady while I read it!"

"Everything okay in'a there, girls?" Rose's dad called from the living room.

"Fine," Mama D told him. "Rosa got a letter from Johnny,

thats'a all!"

"Well? What's he got'a say?" her husband hollered back, in his signature heavy Italian accent.

"We can't a'know, Vito. Rosa say it's a'private! Now, let'a girl read'a her letter!"

Everyone knew that would be the end of the conversation for Vito. Nobody, and I mean *nobody*, defied Mama D, not even her big, tough-talking husband. As Rose silently read her letter, Mama D stood facing her and holding her daughter's trembling wrists.

*

Dear Rose ~

It's only been a week, but it seems like forever. They told us we'd better write letters when we can because things are supposed to get more rigid, and we won't have as much time. We also heard that it'll take longer for our mail to get to us than for our letters to get home to you. Something about all stateside military mail goes to one place and is then sorted and rerouted to different bases. I haven't got a letter from you yet, and I'm sure that's why. The guys have only just started getting letters at mail calls. It's like waiting to receive a golden ticket. When the mailbag is empty, the guys with no envelopes look like kids at Christmas that Santa forgot.

But I've got a lot to hold onto that will get me through. I can still remember the smell of your hair. It's what I think about when I wake up each day, even before the sun comes up. I don't know what I ever complained about at home when my dad had me mowing the lawn at 7 am on a Sunday. That would be like a holiday here. When we get to boot camp, I heard that we'll forget what sleep was like, so I guess I'll look at reveille like a gift for now since it means I got some sleep, anyway. Besides, when I open my eyes, I think of you, so doing it earlier just means I get to think of you longer each day.

Rose, I know our time apart will pass quickly. Just know that I love you and that when I get back, we'll be married and will never again be apart, not even for a day.

Loving You Always,

Johnny

*

"He's a'good? Everything a'fine?" Mama D asked when her daughter relaxed again, and she let go of Rose's wrists.

"Yes, he's good, Mama. Says they get up earlier than ever, and that the guys all say it'll get harder for everyone in the next few weeks." Rose folded the letter and slipped it into her skirt pocket.

"Eh, Johnny will be a'good!" Rose's dad called out from behind his newspaper in the living room. "That'a kid is'a tough. He was a hell of a foot'aball player. He's a'ready for whata'ever they'a throw at a'him!"

Her dad's baritone voice had always comforted Rose, even

when she was a little girl. If Papa D said things would be fine, then his daughter always breathed easier. Rose and Mama D smiled at each other and shook their heads. Vito could be quiet when told to be, but he wouldn't miss out on anything under his roof. Mama D flipped her bread loaf from its hot pan onto a wire cooling rack as Rose rushed to her bedroom to write back to Johnny.

*

My Dearest Johnny,

I just got your letter, and it made my day! Since you mentioned the smell of my hair, I'm sending the enclosed lock of my hair, tied in ribbon. Know that I kissed it and held it to my heart before putting it into the envelope. I hope you can feel me with you whenever you hold it. I guess you've now got another piece of me—besides my heart, I mean.

I already miss you like crazy, and I'm counting the days until you're home again. My parents say the time will move faster than we think. So just imagine it, Johnny—one day, it will be you and me telling our daughter to have faith and hold on until her love returns home to her.

I'm so excited for our future. We'll have a whole houseful of kids! I can see us now on Christmas mornings around our tree, and with four or five little Johnnys, all wearing matching pajamas. It's all I've ever wanted—to be your wife and to have your children.

That day can't get here soon enough. So, Johnny, you stay safe and come home to me. We've got big plans, you and me. Stay safe, love.

Eternally,

Rose

*

As soon as she'd finished writing her letter, Rose sprayed perfume on it, folded it, and slipped into a light-pink envelope along with her lock of hair, tied in a thin pink satin ribbon. She licked a three-cent stamp, affixed it to the envelope, and then ran to put the letter in her family's mailbox outside.

"What's a hurry?" Mama D laughed. "The mailman's already come today! He won't be a'back until tomorrow!"

"You're right," Rose agreed. "I can run it down to the post office and still make today's mail! I'll be back in a few minutes!"

And with that, Rose flew out the front door and, in her skirt and blouse, jogged the few blocks to the local post office. She was eager to get the letter to Johnny as fast as possible.

"Those'a two kids!" Rose's dad Vito laughed, without opening his eyes from his favorite napping spot on his burgundy chenille sofa.

"Right?" Mama D laughed from the kitchen. "Remember how'a we were, Vito? Ah! Amore! It's a beautiful thing! Could no love that'a boy more if he were our own'a son! Wait'll we have grandchildren running around here! Ah, la dolce vita!"

Everyone seemed to feel the same about Johnny. He was just the type of young man most parents wanted for their daughters. In fact, several parents in the neighborhood had tried to push their daughters and Johnny together. He'd always been polite and respectful to them all, but Johnny only had eyes for Rose. She was his, and Johnny was hers, plain and simple. It was how life was meant to be. When the two were together, all was right with the universe and life felt full of promise.

Being apart was difficult for Rose and hard on Johnny, too. But military life kept Johnny busy, which he felt was a blessing. The demanding schedule and physical regimen kept his mind occupied and helped the time pass faster. Plus, when he fell into his bunk at the end of a long day of training, he was always so exhausted he would fall asleep the minute his head hit the pillow.

Meanwhile back at home, Rose continued her high school classes and tried to focus on her studies. But her thoughts always wandered to Johnny. She even got in trouble a few times for daydreaming during class.

"Pardon me, Rose," one teacher said. "Would you mind breaking away from thoughts of your handsome soldier and rejoining us as we discuss the Constitution?" The other students laughed and snickered, but they all liked Rose, and most had known Johnny, too, and were his friends as well.

As the calendar pages flipped, Rose watched the nightly news reports of the war. Then, one evening, she picked up the front page of the *Daily News* in her living room and read the latest. She remembered Johnny's reaction when they heard of the attack on Pearl Harbor. He had immediately announced that he was joining the war effort, and Rose had instantly felt terrified that she could lose him.

As the weeks and months passed, Johnny's letters arrived more sporadically. Since she lived for his letters, Rose wondered how she'd even breathe on the days she didn't receive one. Johnny told her in one letter:

*

We're shipping out soon, and I think it'll be pretty hard to write regularly, so I just wanted to get this last letter in the mail before we head out. We don't have orders yet about where we'll be going, but I'm ready, though. Don't you worry about me, Rose. Boot camp has prepared all of us. I'm just ready to get out there and do my duty and then get back home to you.

*

He was right. His letters arrived less frequently, and sometimes, after no letters for weeks, several of his letters came all at once. Rose's parents also breathed sighs of relief when Johnny's letters arrived. Mama D and Papa Vito had always felt like Johnny was a son. Having him as Rose's husband one day would please them to no end. As far as they'd been concerned, no other young man measured up to Johnny.

"With'a Johnny in God'aforsaken no place, with'a no time'a to write, and then try to get'a the letter into the mail, it all'a take'a much time," Rose's dad reminded her whenever she felt anxious that she hadn't heard from Johnny.

As Rose watched the war unfold through radio broadcasts and newspapers, worry grew, and she tossed and turned through countless sleepless nights. "The Bataan Death March!" Rose said as she sat one night at the dinner table with her face firmly planted in the evening edition of the newspaper. "My God! Did you read this? American and Filipino soldiers forced to march over sixty-five miles after they surrendered, and God knows what they did to the ones who didn't die during the march! I keep thinking of that, and I can't imagine if that were to happen to Johnny! It's so hard not knowing where he's been sent! I don't know if he's taking part in what's in the newspapers or if he's in an even more terrifying situation! I can't take this!"

Mama D and Vito glanced at each other. They both worried but were also concerned that the anxiety was eating away at their daughter, too. It was hard for them to see their girl so frightened.

"Let'a no think those a'things," Mama D told Rose as she served dinner. "That'a stuff you read about should'a no happen. Never. And will no happen again. That'a is a war crime. Japan will pay a'for that. Right is a'right."

"Mama, non si parla di guerra." Vito gently interrupted as he pried the newspaper from Rose's grip. "No more talk'a of war. Okay? Time'a to eat! Mangia!"

But Rose couldn't care less about dinner. And she certainly didn't need a news headline to find a way to inject Johnny into a conversation. "Isn't it funny that Johnny always loved to eat this cold, when everyone else likes it hot?" Rose laughed as she fought back the lump in her throat. Her parents laughed, too, at the memory of how Johnny never wanted to eat the *pizzagaina* dish *hot* like the rest of them.

"Ugh! Johnny! Johnny! Johnny!" Lily, Rose's younger sister, blurted out.

Since Johnny had left for the army, Rose's sister and her brother, Anthony, had felt like second-class citizens, since the dinner conversation was always dominated by talk of the war, Johnny, or Rose and Johnny. They didn't resent their sister, though, and they both loved Johnny like a brother. All three of Mama D and Vito's kids were close. They were all three close in age, so they'd grown up doing most of the same things and hung around the same people in the neighborhood.

"Can't we just once have dinner without talk about Johnny and this dumb war?" a frustrated Lily voiced.

"Please, a' Lily, not a'now," said Papa Vito.

Rose calmly interjected, "Well, excuse me if my Johnny, who's risking his life fighting a godforsaken evil that threatens to take away life as we know it just so you can sit comfortably in your home and eat your damn pizzagaina, without bombs blowing your head off, is a constant topic of discussion that disturbs you. I'm sorry. Please forgive me. But in case you haven't realized, this is much bigger than just Johnny, Lily. This is about our lives. Not only mine and Johnny's, but yours too. It's about the future of our country. The future of the entire world, for crying out loud! And if you don't think that your future, and our freedom, is reason enough to talk about this *dumb war*, as you call it—at dinner, or breakfast, or lunch, or whenever—then you're obviously a fool and don't understand what's really at stake here. And I feel very, very sorry for you." Rose calmly stood up and excused herself from the table.

A sober silence fell over the dining room. Lily quickly realized the impact of what she had said and chased Rose to apologize. Mama D soon followed them both to ensure the peace between her daughters. Papa Vito frustratedly dropped his fork on his plate, sat back in his chair, and released a disheartened sigh. He glanced over at Anthony, expecting him to chime in on the matter.

"What?" said Anthony. "I got nothin' to say. I'm just here for the pizzagaina."

*

Rose's vigil for Johnny was never-ending as she prayed for his safety every day, sometimes three or four times. She was ready to marry her soldier and start their life together. But while most other high school seniors excitedly graduated, Rose only went through the motions, never entirely immersing in the graduation activities and celebrations. She accepted her diploma, moved her tassel on her cap, took the obligatory family photos, and constantly pined for Johnny.

Rose tried not to worry whenever she read news reports showing kamikaze aircraft flying into battleships. She wrapped her arms around herself tightly and held her elbows to stave off the building nausea she felt. Such scenes were often replayed in her dreams.

"My God! These people are crazy! They have nothing to lose!" Rose cried as she nervously rocked back and forth in her seat. "Is this insanity really happening?"

But the jarring newspaper articles and news footage only kept coming. Headlines read, SEA SHOWDOWN, US & JAPANESE FLEETS LOCKED IN BITTER BATTLE, and US CARRIER LOST IN PHILIPPINES.

"I just want to know where he is!" Rose cried. "I need to know that he's safe!"

Her father sat next to his daughter on the sofa, gently coaxed the newspaper from her hands, and handed it to Mama D. She kept quiet this time, but only because she fought back tears as her heart ached for Rose and what she was going through.

"Rosa," Vito said as he wrapped an arm around his daughter's shoulder, "this is'a no good for you. It's a'not how Johnny wants you spendin' a'time. Just say a'your prayers, my girl. God a'will get'a you both a'through, and he'll be a'back to you a'soon."

"You're right, Papa" Rose agreed. "I don't even know where Leyte Gulf is. He may not even be there. Right? I need to stop worrying, or I'll go completely insane."

To calm herself, Rose went to her room and pulled out her pale pink stationery.

*

My Dearest Johnny,

Everyone here is so proud of you. We watch the news and read the articles, and it all looks horrific. With thirty countries involved, I'd think the army could spare you and send you back to me. But then, I know you wouldn't leave, even if they said you could. I understand. I know it's a matter of honor, and I love that about you.

We're seeing that lots of the casualties have been civilians. I hope you haven't seen anything too awful. I saw that the Western Allies have invaded German-occupied France. The photos are almost too much to take. I look for your face in any pictures that come out. My parents want me to stop watching and reading so much, but they're my only link to you. I only wish I knew where you are. I take comfort in the fact that we both *see the same moon and the same sun, but I want to look at them with you beside me. Hugging my pillow is the only way I can get any sleep now, and it's only for a couple hours at a time. It's those times that I hope to dream of you.*

Well, I should go. Please stay safe—and since you say you've left your heart with me, know that I'm keeping it safe over here. Good night, my love.

Eternally,

Rose

*

Rose tried hard to listen to her parents and not worry. But she froze and held her breath one evening when a dark sedan slowly turned onto her street. Everyone in Inwood held their breath when a car like that drove by, ominously snaking through the streets and looking for the family it would destroy. People exhaled when it silently rolled past their homes to ferret out the next victims of the war. The sight was a sickening reminder that one of Inwood's own was not coming home.

Rose had learned that the military generally advised families of a serviceman's death between 5:00 p.m. and midnight. She regularly lost her appetite for dinner and held her breath as she prayed that the familiar dark-colored sedan would never arrive at Johnny's parents' home during those hours. If they got a phone call, she had learned that it would mean that Johnny had been injured. But Rose knew that when the death car came, it was so much worse. Two uniformed soldiers would step from it to deliver a soldier's formal death notification that would implode a family. Rose had even learned that one soldier would give the earth-shattering death notification and that the other soldier, a chaplain, would console the shocked, bereaved family. Since she'd learned how the military did it, Rose prayed even harder for Johnny's safety. And every time a dark sedan rolled through Inwood, Rose silently prayed and bargained with God as she willed the death car to stay away from Johnny's house on Walcott Avenue.

Rose kept every letter Johnny wrote to her and read them again and again every day. She kept all of them wrapped in a red ribbon and inside a jewelry box in her closet. She'd also saved many newspaper articles she'd read, and she planned to give them to Johnny when he returned.

By 1945, the reports became more encouraging, and in May, after six years, the Nazis surrendered, and the war in Europe came to an end. And finally, on August 14, Rose's prayers were answered. "Mama! *Mama!* He's coming home! Johnny's coming home!" Rose screamed when she burst into the house, holding up the latest newspaper headline in her hands: *JAPAN SURRENDERS.* At long last, this tragic world war was over, and a grateful nation celebrated.

CHAPTER 4

"Welcome home, soldier!" the cabbie in a plaid driving cap said as he looked at Johnny in his rearview mirror. "See any action over there?" But Johnny didn't want to talk about his war stories. He was home. He'd done what he'd needed to do, and now it was time to return to his Rose—to his future.

"Yeah, I saw some, that's for sure," Johnny said to the cabbie, but that was all he offered. He held the lock of Rose's hair, tied in the thin pink ribbon, and rolled it between his fingers. He'd done it so many times that he'd sometimes wondered how the hair was still intact. Finally, he slipped it into its worn envelope and tucked it in his pocket. He felt nervous, though he silently chided himself for it. Rose's letters had always said she loved him and was eternally his, but Johnny had been away for a while and couldn't help but worry that some other guy had somehow managed to swoop in and sweep her off her feet.

"Am I drivin' you back to your family's home or to a wife, soldier?" the cabbie asked.

"To my wife—or rather my *future* wife." Johnny smiled.

He'd wanted to surprise Rose, so he hadn't told her what day he'd be back in Inwood. She'd only known the approximate date, and he'd told her he'd let her know more when he could. But as the cab approached her family's home, Johnny hoped Rose would be there, since she'd told him she'd taken a seamstress job to help with the war effort.

The cab drove past the church down the street from Rose's house, the one where Johnny wanted to marry her. As it approached the two-story house on the corner, Johnny craned his neck to look for signs that someone was home.

"Thanks, GI!" the cabbie said as he leaned over the back seat and extended a handshake. Johnny politely took his hand and shook it firmly. But preoccupied, Johnny was eager to sprint up to Rose's front porch and see the only face that mattered to him, the one whose image he'd held onto for so long.

"It was an honor, sir," Johnny said to the cabbie as he opened his door and then stepped out. Before he shut the door, he heard "Johnny! Oh, my God! Johnny!" and saw Rose running toward him from down the street. She dropped her pocketbook and the grocery bag she'd been carrying and ran full speed toward Johnny. He ran toward her and scooped her in his arms, lifted her off the ground, and swung her around.

"You're home! You're back! My God! Is it real, Johnny? Is it really you?" Rose sobbed while she hung onto him and kissed him.

As Rose and Johnny tearfully hugged and laughed, neighbors came out onto their porches, cars stopped, and pedestrians stood frozen as they watched the scene. When Johnny passionately kissed Rose, applause erupted all around, and whistles filled the air. Rose kissed him back like she never had before. For the first time, Rose didn't care who saw or what Mama might say. But when she turned toward her house, Mama D and Papa Vito were also clapping as tears streamed down their faces, too. Their hometown hero had returned safely, their daughter would be getting married, and they'd soon gain a fine son-in-law. All was well in Inwood as far as the DeFabrizio family was concerned.

"Just like I promised!" Johnny laughed, in between kisses. "Our forever starts now! You are eternally my Rose!"

The two young lovers clung tightly to each other, each silently vowing to never let the other go. Neither had ever been so happy or so hopeful for their future.

"Wait, the cab driver!" Johnny remembered, as Rose wiped lipstick off his cheeks with her thumbs. "Let me pay him so he can get outta here."

"I'm not letting go of you again," Rose said as she linked

her arm through Johnny's elbow while he pulled cash from his billfold.

"Oh, no, sir," the cabbie protested as he put up his palms toward Johnny. "This one's on me, son. Welcome home! Now you go and make a happy life for you and the future missus! You've earned it, and we thank you."

Rose saw that even the cabbie had tears in his eyes.

Johnny shook his hand and thanked him, but he couldn't take his eyes off Rose as she held onto his arm and leaned into him.

"I hope there weren't eggs in that bag." Johnny laughed when he nodded down the sidewalk to where Rose's bag and pocketbook lay.

"Eggs? You've been gone for too long." Rose laughed. "Your sweet sister Celia still brings eggs over here all the time from your parents' chickens. We love it, and so does Celia!"

"Celia!" Johnny remembered as he smacked his forehead. "I promised her that I'd come straight to her as soon as I set foot in Inwood."

"What're we waitin' for?" Rose said. "Let's go and see your second-biggest fan!"

"Don't tell Celia that, Rose. She'll fight you for that title."

After Johnny said hello to Mama D and Papa Vito, he told them he needed to go and see Celia and his family.

"Want'a me to drive you? Or you can'a take'a my car," Vito told Johnny.

"Nah, I'd rather walk, but thank you anyway, Mister D. I'll come back and grab my bag later if that's okay."

"Good! Bring your appetite, Johnny!" Mama D called. "Make'a your favorite! You look'a like you never see a full a'meal in a month'a.

*

Twenty minutes later, Johnny and Rose walked hand in hand down the sidewalk toward his family's house. A young boy ran to the edge of his yard to salute the tall, uniformed soldier in the shiny black shoes. Johnny returned the boy's salute.

"Wow! Is he Marco's kid?" he asked Rose.

"Yeah, looks just like his daddy, right? He's about three, I think." She laughed. "I can't wait to see our son, who will look just like his daddy, too!"

Johnny wasn't sure if he should mention any more about Marco. It was common knowledge that Johnny and Marco had been rivals in high school. Ever since Johnny had beat out Marco for a spot on the football team, Marco had despised him. But it wasn't just the football issue. Marco had a long history of jealousy when it came to Johnny. He'd always wanted whatever Johnny had.

"Guess Marco finally gave up tryin' with you, huh?" Johnny finally said.

It was a rhetorical question, and he didn't expect any confirmation from Rose.

But she laughed and said, "I don't think he had much choice. When Mia got pregnant, his fate was pretty much sealed."

Johnny thought about it for a minute and then shook his head. "Poor Mia. Marco's always had eyes for you, and she's always known it. It'd be awful to feel like someone's second choice and that you had to settle for being second best."

"Well, Mia's stuck with *him* and I'm with *you*," Rose said as she squeezed Johnny's hand. "That's all that really matters."

Neither spoke of it, but both remembered when Marco had challenged Johnny to fight outside their high school years earlier. It had started because Johnny told Marco to back off Rose and stop flirting with her. But Marco had felt embarrassed to be dressed down in front of a dozen friends, and since he never settled anything with decorum or tact, no one was surprised when Marco tore off his shirt and then shoved Johnny. All the students parted and gave them space as Johnny and Marco stalked each other like two lions in the wild about to fight over a lioness.

"Marco, I'm tellin' you, man. You're makin' a mistake!" Johnny had warned him. "You don't wanna do this! You may think you can bird dog my girl, but you'll regret this!"

"Oh, the great Johnny Mastantuono is warning me? Now, that's rich! Come on, Johnny! I wanna show Rose what a real man looks like! This is a beatdown you'll never forget!"

But Marco had always been more mouth than muscle, and

this time it would be no different. He took a few jabs, but Johnny was quicker and stronger than Marco. Johnny bobbed and weaved, so his mouthy opponent never even connected with him. But when Marco grabbed Johnny's shirt and torn off a button, Johnny erupted like a long-dormant volcano that threatened to drown everyone in molten lava. Rose knew Johnny was enraged since she had given him the shirt as a gift. But Johnny saw red and flew into a blind fury as he repeatedly pummeled Marco with his fists.

The crowd of students grew, and people cheered on Johnny, hoping to see him annihilate the mouthy Marco. By the time a dean came to break up the fight, Marco was on his back, and Johnny was kneeling on him and punching him without mercy as the students hooted and hollered.

"Break it up! Right now! That's enough, Mr. Mastantuono!" the dean yelled as he pulled Johnny off the bloodied, dazed Marco. "What got into you? This isn't like you!"

"He broke my fuckin' nose!" Marco said through bloodied teeth and swollen lips as he gingerly touched his rearranged face. "It's broke! My nose is broke! What the—"

"I told you not to start with me or else you'd regret it!" Johnny hollered. "I don't start fights, but I always finish 'em! Lemme know when you want some more! I got plenty more for ya!"

"Boys! Enough!" the dean yelled. "Both of you, to my

office! Now!"

Johnny thought he'd be expelled for sure. But when the dean heard that Marco had shoved him and been the instigator, he softened to Johnny. Besides, Johnny had always been a respectful, decent student and never been in trouble.

"Son, listen. You're a good kid. You've never been in this office before, and I don't expect I'll see you again. Do we understand each other?" the dean said.

"Yes, sir. Thank you." Johnny stood up and left, but not before shooting a glare at Marco.

Since Marco had started the fight, only to be bested and humiliated by Johnny, the dean didn't treat Marco quite so favorably. Marco's reputation for being a troublemaker preceded him.

"Detention. Three days, Marco! You need to think about what you want out of your life. Fighting over girls isn't the best way to get it, I can assure you, son!"

After that day, Marco steered clear of Johnny, but the two still always glared at each other and stared each other down in the halls at school. It was common knowledge that they'd never be friends, and that was why Johnny had asked his buddies to keep an eye on Marco for him while he was overseas. Marco saw Rose as Inwood's coveted grand prize. Some thought he would have done anything to win her, since it would mean defeating Johnny, the golden boy. Nothing seemed too diabolical for Marco.

*

As they neared Johnny's family home, Rose and Johnny saw Celia right where she was every afternoon, sitting on her front stoop and waving at people as they drove or walked by. The huge smile never left Celia's sweet face, and an enthusiastic wave from her made everyone's day. She was as much a fixture around Inwood as the old Italian men who'd been around long before Celia had even been born.

Her arm went up, and she waved, but Celia's eyes grew wide when she saw that it was Johnny walking up the sidewalk toward their house. She shot upright and began jumping up and down as she clasped her hands over her mouth, unable to contain her excitement.

"Aaaahhh! Johnny! Johnny, you're *back*! You came back just like you said!" Celia screamed as she ran into her brother and wrapped her arms around him.

"Yep! Came back to see my best girl!" he said as he winked at Rose over Celia's shoulder, holding her tight.

Rose was teary-eyed once again as she watched her future sister-in-law's unbridled happiness. Then, suddenly, Celia released Johnny and leaned back to look at his face.

"Wait! Wait right here, Johnny!" she said as she turned and ran into the house. Johnny thought she was going inside to get their parents. But only seconds later, Celia ran back outside with a box in her hands.

"I did just what you asked, Johnny. I looked after all your

cards, and I didn't even open the most important ones," she reported proudly. "I even slept with the box on my bed every night, just to keep an eye on it."

"I knew you'd be the one to take care of them for me." Johnny smiled. "I can always count on you, Celia."

"You sure can. I'm your best girl. Right, Johnny?" she beamed.

CHAPTER 5

"Frank? Hey, Frank!" Ma called from inside the house. I'd just dozed off while listening to the relaxing wind chimes. I thought there was no way she could be finished telling the long and winding story about events that had taken place decades earlier. I was sure Ma would stretch it out for Debbie, who'd never heard all the specific details, and that she would add the appropriate pauses to allow for Debbie's anticipated shocked gasps.

"Frank, c'mere!" Ma called, louder this time and with more insistence.

"Yeah, Ma. Coming!" I said, with my eyes still shut. I got up begrudgingly, ever the obedient son and only child of my parents, Lena and John. In a traditional family, or even an Italian American family, it doesn't matter how old a son is, he does not *ever* ignore or disobey his mother.

"Frank, can you put on a fresh pot for me? Debbie would like a fresh cup of coffee," Ma said when I walked back inside.

"Sure, Ma. No problem."

"Oh, and while you're standin' around waitin' on it to be done percolatin', can you bring the Stella D'oro on the counter there? And grab some plates."

"Yeah, Ma, okay. I got it," I said from behind her, as Debbie fought to contain her laughter that I instantly reverted to the obedient son, thrown back in time to when I'd been a boy. Debbie knew I'd never disobey my mother, no matter how old I was. It was how I'd been raised, and I had never questioned it. We respected our mothers, and we defended their honor. Besides, I'd always fiercely loved Ma, even before I understood more about the woman who was my mother.

As a little boy, I didn't pay as much attention to how my parents had interacted. But right around junior high, I got to a point where I noticed a quiet sadness in her eyes, one that I realized had always been there, even when I'd been too young to identify it. Sure, Ma had always smiled with her mouth, but her eyes had hidden something more, something I never could understand.

Ma had always been a good, God-fearing woman who had placed her family first. She'd been the glue that had held our family together in good times and in bad. My mother was the calm in a storm and the safe harbor for all of us. I know it's like that in most families, but as I got older, Ma seemed even stronger than other mothers, almost like she possessed some unseen superhuman strength she drew upon when necessary.

Ma was reliable, dependable, and even predictable. She was attractive but in a sensible, respectable sort of way. Ma had always been a simple, nice-looking woman with darker auburn hair and nice skin, but not in a sexy, alluring way. She was the sort of girl parents would want for their sons. She offered stability, fidelity, and a solid foundation, while not being so over-the-top pretty that she'd attract attention that could make waves in a marriage.

My father had always seemed to love her, yet I never felt the temperature rise in the room when Dad came home from work and laid eyes on Ma. I never came in unexpectedly and found my parents in an awkward moment or a playful embrace. My dad never came home and laid a passionate kiss on Ma that took her breath away. As a boy, I didn't notice such things. Yet as I grew older and started noticing girls, I realized that such a component might be missing between my parents.

Dad was a good man and had always been for his whole life. He was raised with his Italian family's Old World values to respect others and treat them as he preferred to be treated. Unlike some in Inwood, my dad wasn't an opinionated, prejudiced sort who thought himself better than other races or religions. He believed in a fair day's pay for a hard day's work and never asked anyone for anything. He was an honorable man who'd earned his own way his whole life. My father was a prideful man whose handshake was his bond. Most people in our neighborhood were the same way. Because of it, crime in our town could be measured by stolen bicycles.

"Use the Chock Full o' Nuts, Frank!" Ma called from the living room.

"I know, Ma! The company coffee. I got it!" Ma had raised me to know that when company stopped by, often unannounced, we should always pull out the better china, the good coffee, and of course the staple of every Italian American kitchen—Stella D'oro. Being a gracious host, and making people feel welcome, was her nature. I'd heard Ma and my aunts have thirty-minute conversations about a fifteen-minute visit at someone's home. Why china patterns mattered was beyond me, but this need to be the hostess with the mostest was a quiet competition between women in the neighborhood. I presumed there was some score pad someplace where they tallied up their hostess abilities.

I guess the men in my family had their own club with its own unwritten rules. Dad and my uncles often sat around talking about the war, the Yankees, or who got a new lawnmower. The men didn't seem to compete, not like the women. The men were simply exchanging news and sharing opinions.

"And bring the cubes!" Ma added. "The *sugar* cubes!"

"Already got 'em!" I rolled my eyes, but only because I was out of Ma's sight. God forbid we should offer a guest *granulated* sugar instead of the fancy cubes and the delicate sugar tongs. But I must admit that I had always appreciated Ma's attention to detail and that she liked to uphold her standards. She used to tell me, "You teach others how to treat *you*, Frankie. It's by how you hold yourself, how you communicate and regard others, and the character you show to the world. Lets 'em know what they can expect from you."

I understood what Ma meant. As I grew older, I watched as she painted on her lipstick as if to remind herself to smile and put on a happy face for all the world to see. But she sometimes dabbed at the edges of her eyes when she thought no one noticed, and I'd seen Ma pull back her shoulders and swallow down her pride more times than I could count. It hurt me to see her try so hard to be happy, only to settle in life.

When the percolator had finished, I put the carafe on a tray where I'd already placed the Stella D'oro biscotti, two coffee cups, and a bowl of sugar cubes, along with my grandmother's special sugar tongs. Ma's parents had left behind many heirlooms and keepsakes when they arrived from Italy, so she treasured the few items she still had and proudly used them whenever we had company.

When I carried the tray into the living room, I tried not to look at Debbie, lest I crack a smile about being Ma's obedient houseboy. But Debbie knew what it was like to have an Italian American mom.

"Piping-hot coffee to keep this party going," I said as I placed the tray on a coffee table between Ma and Debbie.

"What? Only two cups? You're joining us, right?" Ma asked.

"Um, nah. I'll sit this one out. You two go ahead, and you tell Debbie the story. In fact, I think you'll be a while, so I'm gonna go and lie down in the back bedroom."

"Eh, suit yourself," Ma sighed as she waved her hand and dismissed me.

Going through the whole decades-old story always exhausted me. I'd processed the ins and outs of it for years. It had kept me up at night and plagued my daytime hours, too, for so long. Every time I got a few answers, new questions also developed, and I got bogged down in the whole thing. But getting details from my dad was even worse than pulling teeth. I'd heard that he'd once been talkative and gregarious, that guy who was always the life of the party. But after *it* happened, he had withdrawn into himself and pulled away from life and people for the first time. It seemed to me that Dad had closed himself off from everyone and everything.

I kicked my shoes off and flopped on my back onto Ma's

guest bed in the immaculate bedroom that rarely got used anymore. The beige and orange afghan she crocheted was at my feet, so I pulled it up around my shoulders. Surrounded by the scents of home and many of the pictures and knickknacks of my youth, I soon drifted off to sleep.

I suppose that since my mom was talking about it, I had the story on my mind as I nodded off. In no time, Ma's voice got quieter in the living room. I fell deeply into a dream that replayed the whole story, yet again, as if I were watching an old Super 8 film reel. Nonetheless, as I drifted off, my mind paid attention to all the details and particulars I had come to know about how it had unfolded and impacted so many people in our small town.

*

"It was good, Lena," Dad told my mom that night, after silently eating his dinner while Ma and I talked about my day and my plans for the weekend. We'd tried to engage my dad, but as usual, he seemed lost in his own thoughts and uninterested in our dinner conversation. I didn't mind so much for myself, but I wished he would engage with Ma and pay her more attention. She always spent so much time and effort preparing our meals and keeping the house. She deserved some conversation and interaction with her husband.

"Glad you enjoyed it," Ma said just like she did every night, but with a hint of hollow sadness in her tone.

Without another word, Dad pushed his chair back from the table and then headed predictably toward the basement door. For as long as I could remember, my dad had kept the same routine. Ma said he liked to go down to the basement and work with his tools just to relax. I never understood how one *works* to relax, but I didn't question my mom.

The basement was Dad's domain, an early sort of man cave, before such a place had the moniker. He used the basement as a woodworking shop. He even had some of his dad's old lathes and hand tools hanging from a pegboard along a wall. Ma and I rarely ventured beyond cracking the door and calling downstairs to him when he was needed.

I'd always loved the smells in the basement. An amalgamated mix of powerful scents, including wood shavings, oils, and stains, the basement took on a life of its own that was entirely separate from the rest of our home. It looked and smelled different, and even had an unsettling vibe of its own, unlike the rest of our home. Whenever we opened the basement door, the scents from below drifted up and briefly washed over us. But Ma and I never ventured down into the basement. That was my father's space, his place to go, relax, and unwind after a hard day's work. At least, that's what I'd always thought while growing up in our house.

Honestly, I'd thought as a kid that my parents were just like everyone else's. In many ways, my family was like everyone else's family. Ma took care of home and hearth, and Dad went to work each day like clockwork to provide for our family. When it was time to eat, Ma came outside and called for me, as the other boys' moms did.

"Comin', Ma!" I always replied as soon as I heard her call for me.

But one day, when I handed the bat to my buddy and ran toward home, one of the other eight-year-old boys scoffed, "*Ma!* Huh! Right! She's not even your real mother!"

I looked at him like he was crazy and then ran toward Ma, where she waited.

"Frankie, what's goin' on?" Ma asked when I got to her. "What'd he say to you?"

I wasn't sure if I should even vocalize it, but Ma urged again.

"What? Tell me, Frankie."

"He said you're not my real mom."

"Don't listen to those boys. Come on; I've got your favorite waitin' on the table."

Years passed, but I still thought of that comment every so often. I could have asked my friend what he'd meant, but something told me to just *let it alone*, as Ma said about things she never wanted to discuss. One afternoon, when I was grown, I came home for dinner as I did a few times a week. My mother was outside watching Dad aggressively dig in the garden with a spade. They weren't talking. Ma just stared at him as if contemplating something.

"What were you just thinkin' about, John?" Ma asked.

As if shaken from his thoughts, Dad said, "How much I hate the sight of these dead plants out here."

But Ma didn't seem satisfied with his answer as she postured and continued to eye Dad with her hands on her hips. Finally, after a few minutes, she sighed, shook her head, and came inside the house. I wondered if maybe I'd walked in on something between my parents. Yet there would be no way I'd find out anything from my dad, that was for sure. He'd grown even quieter over the years. He went to work, came home, and preferred to keep to himself.

"Smells good in here, Ma!" I said as I kissed her on the cheek.

Her face lit up just like it had for my whole life when I kissed her hello. I'd made it my job to make my mother's face light up and smile. I could tell she needed to feel appreciated and noticed, and Ma was a good woman. She deserved to be happy. But as much as I'd tried over the years, Ma's smile had always seemed the tiniest bit forced, as if she'd smiled only to make me feel better, not because her heart felt happy and full. I could tell it wasn't a genuine smile, not one she felt all the way to her soul. Ma was like that. She wanted others to feel good and to be happy, but she'd always put her feelings last, as if hers didn't matter as much.

As I grabbed a spoon to taste her sauce on the stove, my

dad came inside and placed a big red tomato on the countertop. Silently and intently, he washed his hands at the kitchen sink and then dried them on a nearby dishtowel.

"Look at that tomato!" Ma said. "And in October."

"Yeah, a survivor," Dad said.

It was a simple, almost pleasant, moment. But I wouldn't savor it for long before the two started their predictable banter. They'd always been so predictable.

Dad nodded toward the vase of orange and yellow flowers that Ma had finished arranging. I knew he'd say something.

"Lena, why you gotta waste money like that? Couple of bucks down at the new Costco, and you'd get a bigger bunch that'll last forever."

"I wanted *these*, John. I want it to be pretty in here."

Dad just shook his head, pulled a sharp knife from the butcher block, and easily sliced it through the ripe tomato, but with shaking hands. As I watched the juicy liquid spill onto the cutting board, I realized that my parents were also holding onto something within their skins, just as that tomato had done until my father had picked it from the garden.

We ate dinner that night, and Ma asked about my day. She told us that our neighbor had been ill and that her daughter was staying with her. Ma also mentioned she'd been considering making new curtains for the kitchen. Dad didn't respond.

"Whatta you think, John?"

"About what?" Dad asked.

"The curtains, John. Do you think I should make some new curtains?"

"Whatever you think, Lena. It's your kitchen." He shrugged as he pushed his chair back and got up after he'd cleaned his plate.

I didn't look at Ma's eyes. I didn't want to see the sadness that I knew was there. Just like always, I knew that it was up to me to pick up the slack and make her feel better.

"You got the fabric already, Ma?" I asked. "Show it to me later."

I'd done it countless times before. I'd feigned interest to make her feel less invisible and more included. Dad was never actually mean to my mother. It wasn't that at all. He'd just seemed indifferent and unengaged, almost like he couldn't give any more of himself, not even to his wife of several decades, the woman who'd pledged her life to him.

After dinner, my parents sat together on our brown-and-beige floral sofa to watch some TV. They were physically together, but there was an almost visible dividing line between them that reminded me of the Continental Divide. Ma was on one side and Dad on the other. It was just like most other nights in our home.

I knew my dad would head down to the basement when the show had ended. It had become an almost nightly routine, and he'd done it for as long as I could remember. Time had marched on, and they'd gone from a small Admiral black-and-white TV to an RCA color console, but not much else had changed over the years between my parents. Dad might wait for a program to finish before he went downstairs, but he'd always head to the basement steps and shut the door, leaving Ma alone upstairs.

Unable to concentrate on watching TV, my eyes kept going toward the basement door off the kitchen. I rarely heard sounds of hammering, sawing, or sanding coming from the basement when he was down there. Instead, I wondered what the man did with his time, tucked away and blanketed with the earthy scents of woods and oil-based stains.

"Thanks, Ma," I said as I got up from my chair. "I'm stuffed, and I've got an early day tomorrow. So, I'm takin' off."

I leaned over the back of the couch and kissed Ma on her cheek. She patted my face behind her with one hand without taking her eyes off the TV screen. Dad raised his chin in a slight nod to me, and he and Ma sat on the couch with a couple of feet between them. It felt to me like the distance between them might as well have been a hundred miles.

I walked toward the back door, but then my glance fell to the basement door again. I stopped, glanced at the backs of my parents' heads on the couch, and then walked closer to the heavy wooden door with its oil-rubbed metal handle, which had turned dark with age. I just had to know what Dad found so interesting that he hunkered downstairs every night and ignored my mother. With one more glance, I confirmed that they were too engulfed in the TV show in front of them to notice that I was even still there.

The TV's volume was up so high that I knew they'd never hear the soft, telltale squeak of the basement door. The lazy squeak was one of those familiar house sounds that everyone knows but that they hear so much they come to ignore it. I quietly stepped through the doorway and then carefully shut the door behind me, careful not to jiggle the heavy metal knob and arouse attention. As I got to the third wooden step, I pulled an overhead cord to switch on the light below. The basement was dimly lit even with the light on, and shadows stretched up around me as I walked down the last steps. Those familiar aromas of woods, paint stains, and oils hung in the air as my eyes adjusted to my surroundings in the unfinished stale basement.

Dad had a few long-forgotten wood projects on a workbench. So, I picked up a half-finished birdhouse and looked at the mitered corners and the hand-tooled design he had scrolled on the roof. I shook my head and laughed to myself. My father had always been a fine craftsman. Whether he built new stairs or a small birdhouse, my dad always did it right. I could still hear his words from long ago.

"The measure of a man can be seen in all he does, Frank," Dad had said. "What you put out there and show to the world reflects back onto *you*. Don't ever forget that."

As I put the birdhouse back onto the bench, I noticed a thick layer of dust that outlined the square where the birdhouse had sat. Dad obviously hadn't picked it up in quite a while. Beside the bench hung a couple of matching flower boxes he had started years earlier, but when I ran a finger over one, the thick layer of dust showed they hadn't been touched in ages, either. I couldn't imagine what my dad did in his workshop for the life of me since there weren't any other wood projects around.

I walked around, looked at all the old hand tools that hung from a giant peg board over the workbench. I knew some had come from my grandfather and my great-grandfather, just a few items left from generations gone by. Then, finally, my eyes fell to an old, worn black-and-white photograph. When I picked it up from the bench and looked closer, I saw that it was an old photo of a group of teenagers, including one who must be Dad. Based on the wavy hair, chiseled cheekbones, and the signature dimple in his chin, the smiling kid in the photo couldn't be anyone else. He was the only one in the group wearing an army uniform, and a raven-haired beauty leaned into him, posing happily for the photo. It looked like the guys and girls in the picture were inside a club of some sort and seated at a large table. I also recognized Aunt Gina, my Dad's sister, who still lived down the street from my parents.

I couldn't imagine what Dad did in his basement workshop. So much of what was there looked untouched, even forgotten by time. There was another attached room at the end of the basement, and while I was there, I figured I'd have a look. But when I pushed open the door, the contents of the room looked like much of the same. Garden tools hung on a wall, toolboxes sat untouched on a shelf, buckets and paint rollers sat inside two old paint pans, and Dad's old army footlocker sat on the bottom shelf of a gray metal storage rack. There was nothing of interest stored in my parents' basement. Dad didn't even have a TV set or radio in the workshop, just an old turntable record player in a locking case.

I shrugged and shut the door. I decided that maybe he simply enjoyed his solitude and a place to relax and unwind. Since I'd already said goodbye to my parents, I switched off the light and then left out of the door that led to the yard.

"Hey! Frank, wake up," Debbie said from the guest bedroom's doorway. "You've been asleep for hours in here."

I opened my eyes to a darkened room and realized it must be late.

"You and Ma all finished?" I asked as I stretched. "Did she give you the whole story?"

"Boy, did she ever!" Debbie shook her head. "Lena told me the story was even in *Life* magazine. Who knew your family went through such an insane tragedy?"

CHAPTER 6

Years passed after the day I first ventured into my dad's basement workshop. I ultimately married Debbie, got a good job, and we had a son, Paul. When the house next door to my parents' home went up for sale, Ma told me that she thought Debbie and I should look at it.

"Might need a bit of updating, but it's a nice size, and it's got good bones. You two need more space with a young son. And hopefully a girl on the way soon." Ma happily grinned.

Some people might not want to live next door to their parents. For me, however, it seemed like the next step in my life. I'd watched as my dad's sister moved in down the street, along with a couple of cousins. Inwood was comprised of many multigenerational Italian families who'd made their homes there for decades. It was typical for relatives to live within walking distance of one another, if not in the same home, in some cases. We took care of our own, and family always came first. That's just how it was.

Maybe those truths played into how I felt when my marriage to Debbie got rocky in 2000. She said I was demanding, I told her she nagged too much, and neither of us was good at compromise. But I didn't want my marriage to break up. My parents had been together all their lives, and they'd made it work. I didn't want to have a failed marriage, but Debbie grew tired of our constant bickering. So, after an exhaustive three-day argument, I can't say that I was shocked when I arrived home to find Debbie had packed up one day and left me after more than two decades.

A few days passed, and I didn't hear from Debbie. I grew anxious and irritable since it was hard to sleep. Finally, one hot afternoon, I was working on a roofing job when I took a break and called Debbie again. Finally, this time, she answered.

"We're done talkin', Frank," Debbie said.

"How can we be done when you haven't talked to me at all?" I asked. "Where are you stayin' anyhow?"

"Hey! Mista M, can I get some help ova here, please?" my square-jawed helper called as he impatiently gestured with a nail gun.

I ignored him and kept trying to get Debbie to talk to me. But she'd always been a firecracker, and she was over-the-top mad. The sun was high in the sky, and there wasn't a cloud in sight as sweat poured down my face and neck.

"We're *done*, Frank! Over! *Finito!*" Debbie hollered.

"Aww, come on! Now, that's bullshit and you know it! Don't try to play me, Debbie! I'm warnin' you! Don't screw with me!"

"Mista M! Hey, we still got six rows to do before lunch!" Bobby called out as I paced on the searing roof.

"Ayy! What the fuck? Don't ya see I'm on the damn phone over here!" I yelled to him as I held the phone away from my ear.

"Okay now, Debbie, listen to me," I began again.

But all I heard was silence. She'd hung up.

"Damn it!" I yelled as I hurled my phone down hard into the bed of my pickup, where it shattered into pieces.

Bobby and I briefly locked eyes in a tense standoff, but he knew not to test me, not at that moment. Without another word, Bobby lowered his safety glasses and got back to work. Unfortunately, I was sure it would be another sleepless night for me.

A few days later, I decided to confront Debbie in person at her shop. I drove into town and parked near the Hair Today Beauty Salon and waited for her to close up. I checked my watch and knew I'd have to wait a few minutes. But almost like clockwork, Debbie and a small group of stylists stepped out of the salon and said good night to one another while Debbie locked the door. She turned and walked toward her car, and I jumped out of my truck, ran across the street, and walked quickly to catch up to her.

As she unlocked her car and opened the driver's door, she saw me. "Jesus, Frank. You scared the shit out of me." She sighed as she shut her eyes and shook her head. "What d'ya want?" she said as she started to get into her car.

"Twenty-eight years, Debbie. You don't just get to walk away," I said as I held the door open.

"Oh yeah, I do. Because if I stay one more minute, I'm gonna turn into your mutha! And I'd rather slit my wrists than be in her position!" she venomously spat.

"What's wrong with my *mother*?" I asked.

"Your father, Frank! Your father is what's wrong with your mutha! But big surprise! You never noticed *that* either!"

Dumbfounded, I backed up and shut Debbie's car door. She started the engine, threw the car into gear, and squealed her tires as she sped off. Debbie was nothing if not dramatic; it was true. But I was shocked she'd brought my mother into our argument.

I got in my truck and drove home. Minutes later, I parked and decided to walk over and see how Ma was doing. Debbie's comment had rung in my ears all the way home. I thought that I was the only one who had noticed something off with my parents but apparently not.

Since I knew the back door would be open, I walked

around to my parents' backyard. Dad was hoeing in the garden, lost in his thoughts. Ma shook out a bathroom rug as she watched Dad and smiled, obviously hoping to catch his attention. My dad never looked up, and Ma's smile faded as she gave the rug a final, vigorous snap. Defeated, she was turning to go back inside when she saw me.

"Oh! Hi, Frank." Ma smiled with her lips but not her eyes before she stepped into the house.

I was already hyped up after the exchange with Debbie, but I'd had more than I could take of how Dad ignored Ma as if he didn't even see her.

"You got any idea how lucky you are?" I yelled at Dad as I walked closer.

With a smoldering cigarette hanging from the corner of his lips, Dad forcefully slammed the hoe to the ground and glared at me with a piercing stare as he balled up his fists. He may have aged some, but he was still in shape, just as Johnny had been his whole life. He bowed up at me, but I didn't flinch. Years of frustration collided inside me like angry, ominous seas that threatened to drown both of us. The contemptuous furor in Dad's eyes slammed into me like a gut punch that threatened to take my breath away. But Dad got a hold of himself, he bent over to grab his hoe and angrily attacked the garden soil once again.

I turned away from Dad and stormed up the concrete steps to the back door. Before I went inside, I turned and shot him a disgusted look. But he didn't seem to care as he furiously hoed the dead plants from the garden.

"Fix yourself some iced tea, Frank." Ma smiled with her back to me when I walked in. "Hot out there, right?"

"Even hotter a while ago when I tried to talk to Debbie," I snickered as I grabbed the pitcher of tea from the refrigerator and then lingered to enjoy the cold air a bit longer.

"Oh? So, did you talk to her?"

"I don't think you'd call it that, Ma. She did most of the talking."

"Just give it time, Frank. She'll come around eventually."

"You talkin' from experience here, Ma?"

I took a drink of my iced tea and leaned my back against the counter where Ma chopped a cucumber in half on a cutting board. But she didn't answer me. Instead, she only sighed and said, "Go and call your father."

"Look, Ma," I started to say.

"Go and call him, Frankie. I don't want his dinner to dry out."

I knew that tone. Whenever she reverted to calling me Frankie, I knew she meant business. I just rolled my eyes and turned toward the basement door, since I figured Dad would put away his tools before he came upstairs to eat dinner. He was nothing if not predictable. For my whole life, when my dad worked in the yard, he used the basement door to go outside since that was where he kept his tools.

"Where you goin'?" Ma asked. "Just call him out back. Don't go down there."

"I need the *exercise*," I scoffed as I pulled open the door to the basement.

I shut the door behind me and took a few steps down the staircase. Dad wasn't down there, so I figured he hadn't come in from the yard yet. But I noticed the workshop room's door was slightly ajar, and a thin beam of light cut through the dimly lit basement. I walked closer, but just before I reached for the doorknob to go in, I stopped myself. I squinted my eyes and leaned toward the crack in the doorway. As I silently peered inside the storage room with shelves and a workbench, I saw Dad. He was humming an old love song as he looked at a photo.

The army footlocker was pulled forward in its spot on a bottom shelf, and its lid was open. Dad stopped humming and swallowed hard. His head hung sadly as he kissed his two fingers and then touched the photo before replacing it in the old footlocker. I stood unnoticed as Dad then shut the footlocker, rested his hand on top briefly, and then pulled a beat-up tarp over the top of the old storage box.

I quickly turned and ran toward the stairs and then took them two at a time. When I got to the top of the stairs, I turned back and called out, "Dad! Dinner!" I heard the door close at the end of the basement, and Dad's footsteps came closer as I went into the kitchen where my mom was putting the last serving dishes on the table.

"Smells good, Ma," I distractedly said as I tried to process what I had just seen downstairs.

As I washed my hands at the kitchen sink, Dad ascended from the basement and headed to the bathroom down the hall. For the first time, I felt like a stranger in my family home. I'd known my father for all my life, but I had never fully understood him. And now, after I'd witnessed the weird scene downstairs, I felt more confused than ever about the man who was my father and the woman beside him, who seemed content to let him look right through her.

But I would not find any answers at the dinner table. Ma, Dad, and I all ate in silence, each lost in our own thoughts. Minutes later, I sopped sauce from my plate with a chunk of bread and stared at the empty chair where Debbie had sat for over two decades. It seemed odd that in a house where no one and nothing had changed for my whole life Debbie's chair sat empty. The only sounds were of our forks on our plates and the ice cubes occasionally clinking in our glasses. I watched my dad and mom, and I wondered what secrets he'd withheld from my mother. I couldn't bear to think of Ma's feelings getting hurt by whatever she might learn, but it wasn't right that she was in the dark and possibly being deceived. Something just didn't feel right, and I wanted some answers.

After dinner, I stretched out on the couch, in no hurry to

go home to my empty house where I'd only stare at the ceiling all night, unable to sleep. The TV was on, but I wasn't watching it as I thought about what I'd seen in the basement earlier. Finally, Ma switched off the kitchen light and came to join me.

"Did your father go to bed already?" she asked, but it was a rhetorical question that demanded no answer, since Dad had already made his nightly pilgrimage to the basement. So, with that done, there was nothing left for him to do but go to bed, fall asleep, and then wake at dawn to repeat the same things he did every day.

"You gonna sleep at home?" Ma asked. "You know you can sleep here. The guest bed's already made up."

"Yeah, I'm goin' home in a bit. I just wanna find out who did it first," I said as I nodded toward the cop show on TV.

"Mind if I go ahead and go up?" Ma asked as she stood behind the couch.

"Go to bed, Ma," I waved. "And dinner was good as always."

She leaned over the couch and kissed the top of my head. "Night. Lock up when you go home."

"Night, Ma." I craned my neck and watched her climb up the stairs. I gave her time to get into bed, just in case she might come down for a glass of water or something she'd forgotten. While I waited, I stared at the basement door. Finally, after I couldn't take it anymore, I turned up the TV's volume and looked up the stairs to where Ma had turned off the hallway light.

With the TV volume raised to drown out the squeak, I slowly opened the basement door, stepped through, and shut it behind me. I took two steps and pulled the light cord to see to get down the stairs. Unfortunately, the light didn't help much since it was pitch-dark outside, and no moonlight peeked in through the narrow ground-level window. I carefully made my way around the lifetime of stuff my parents had accumulated and stored in the basement. No wonder Ma never went down there. The basement held nothing that would interest my mother. But then, I presumed my dad had been counting on that.

As I passed my old Schwinn bicycle, I remembered how Dad had once taught me to put on a new chain when I was about ten years old. A Christmas tree stand sat on a nearby shelf beside a big ornament storage box and the wreath Ma had always hung on our front door. An old football, slightly deflated, rested on top of a suitcase. I remembered playing catch with my father when I'd been a kid. Sure, I had memories of times spent with my dad. He'd physically been there with me all my life, but I had never felt like he had been *mentally* present and engaged in whatever we did. His mind had always seemed to be elsewhere, like something more important preoccupied him. As I grew from a boy into a man, I decided to endure Dad's stoic, detached demeanor, but

Ma was a different story. I'd always hated how Dad regarded Ma, but since she wouldn't deal with him, I'd long since decided that it was my job to make her feel better whenever I could.

CHAPTER 7

My heart thumped like a runaway jackhammer as my upper lip sweated. My heart sounded so loud that I'd have sworn others could have heard it had I not been alone in the silent, still basement. I reached for the doorknob, wondering if whatever lay on the other side might change everything I'd ever believed. A part of me wondered for a split second if I should just turn and walk away. Ma's advice to leave it alone rang in my head. But then, I knew she couldn't have meant to ignore whatever secrets Dad had tucked away. If Dad was hiding something, she deserved to know.

I swallowed hard and shut my eyes as I turned the knob and opened the door to the workshop at the end of the basement. I switched on the light inside the small room and looked immediately to the bottom shelf to my right. As I squatted down to pull the heavy old tarp off the footlocker, I noticed my hands were shaking. What would I find out? Was Dad hiding some awful secret? Had he been unfaithful to Ma? What did he do down here? I wasn't sure, but I knew the answers were likely at my fingertips.

I pulled off the tarp and slid it to the side, and then I pulled the footlocker toward me so I could open its lid. As I lifted the lid, I saw newspaper clippings, a bunch of old letters in envelopes with handwriting on them, and some photographs. My chest tightened and ached as I pulled out the first news clipping. It was the yellowed front page of the *Daily News*. The headline read, *BRIDE FALLS DEAD IN AISLE TO ALTAR*, and above the article was a photo of a pretty, dark-haired young bride flanked by an older man and woman who I presumed to be the bride's parents. The caption under the photo read *Death walks behind her.* Before I read the article, I noticed a *Life* magazine inside the footlocker, and it was open to a two-page spread with the headline *A BRIDE DIES AT HER WEDDING.*

"What the," I said aloud as I stared in shock at the photo in the magazine. With his thick, wavy hair, chiseled jawline, and telltale chin dimple, there was no mistaking that the young man in the photo was Dad. But who was the bride, and why was she in the same article that had a photo of my father?

There was another news clipping in the footlocker, this

one from the *Daily Mirror* in the UK. The photo showed the same bride inside a casket and surrounded by mourners, including a much younger Dad, who looked heartbroken as he wept while people tried to comfort him. I was so confused, but I remembered how, many years ago, my friend had said, "She's not your real mom" when Ma had come out to call me in for dinner. Could it be true? Was Ma *not* my mother? What did all this mean?

I sat down on the concrete floor to read the articles. But I was left with even more questions after I'd finished. The caption under the funeral photo read, *The End of a Tragic Love Story.* What love story? Who was the bride in the photo? Why did Dad keep these old clippings? Dozens of questions flew about in my head rapid-fire, but I couldn't sort out what I was seeing. None of it made any sense to me.

Many old pink envelopes were rubber-banded together, along with a lock of dark hair tied in a thin ribbon. There was also an album cover that held a vinyl record entitled, *More Than You Know.* I opened a nearby record player case and pulled out the cord. When I looked for an outlet to plug it in, I noticed a coiled extension cord was already plugged into a wall outlet, as if Dad had used it recently. I put the record on the turntable and turned on the portable record player. As it rotated, I gently lifted the needle arm and placed it on the vinyl record.

As Frank Sinatra's voice filled the small workshop, I

suddenly realized it was the same song Dad had been humming when I'd seen him earlier. Nothing made sense—none of it. As the music played, I pulled out the first envelope from the stack and took out the folded letter inside. When I saw the greeting, my breath caught, and I leaned back and sat on the floor.

*

My Dearest Johnny,

Your letter came earlier today, and I think I've read it a dozen times. I can tell from your handwriting that you were in a hurry to dash off a letter to me, so I'm very grateful to have received it. We're watching all the events unfold in the news, but I hope the war ends soon and that you'll come home to me before too long.

Johnny, I'm so excited about our future that I can hardly sleep some nights. I just want you to hold me in your arms again and dream with me about all the children that we'll have someday. Mama predicts we'll have five, but I'll be happy with as many as you want. I hope you'll want to have our first baby soon after we've married because I'm so excited, my love.

Oh, before I forget—your sister Gina brought Celia over yesterday, and Celia is over the moon about going to our wedding. When I told her that we'd like for her to be a part of the wedding, Celia giggled with delight and grinned ear to ear. She's such a special girl. Honestly, I think her so-called "handicap" is truly a gift. I can't wait to call her my sister, Johnny!

Well, since I write to you almost daily, not a lot has changed around here since yesterday. But I wanted to tell you that I think of you every minute of every day. You're my first thought when I open my eyes in the morning and my last thought each night as I say my prayers before bed.

Come home to me safely so we can start our life together, my love!

Eternally Yours,

Rose

*

Johnny. The letters were all written to Johnny, to my father, or the man I had always known to be my father. But who was Rose, this woman who professed her undying love for my father? I shut my eyes to think about what it all meant. Was Rose my mother? Had my young friend known the truth about my mother? Was Lena, the sweet woman sleeping upstairs, not my birth mother? But no, the woman in the newspaper couldn't be my mother, not based on the dates of the newspaper clippings. I'd been born shortly after the articles had been published.

"What the hell is all this?" I whispered as I read another letter with more of the same.

Letter after letter, and none of them gave me any answers. The words were different, but the message was the same. The letter writer was clearly in love with Johnny. I went through envelopes and letters and read the same curly, neat handwriting. Some of the words would be forever ingrained in my memory:

*

...can't wait to sleep next to you every night and wake beside you every morning.

My heart beats for you.

When you take me in your arms, it feels so right..

Our love is for all eternity, Johnny.

...can't wait to be your wife and to have you as my husband.

*

The love letters might have sounded sweet, had they not been written to my dad. The sentiments in the letters would have been fine if they'd been written by Ma. But these were not the realities I held in my hands. In fact, I realized that reality had never been as I'd known it.

"Who *were* these people? Who *are* my parents?" I thought, as I opened the next letter, only to find more of the same. My hands nervously trembled as I read:

*

My hand belongs in yours, and my heart forever belongs to you, too, Johnny.

I'm glad we waited for as long as we did. But when I'm really missing you, I remember our night on the beach. I shut my eyes and recall the warmth and smoothness of your skin and how it feels to trace the muscles on your arms and your stomach.

*

Anger collided with confusion inside me. Nothing made sense—not what was in that basement nor what was in my world. It felt like I was in some alternate universe where my dad had a doppelgänger who'd lived an entirely different life than the father I knew.

"Breathe, Frank. Just breathe," I thought as I stopped reading and looked up at the shadows on the ceiling. My life seemed as unclear as the stretched, overlapping images above me. I needed clarity.

"Okay, lemme think about this." I sighed, as if to clear the cobwebs and uncover the answers. But one question only led to the next.

"Does this mean Rose is my mother?"

"So, who is Ma, then?"

"No, that doesn't work. I'm not as old as the articles. But I'm close."

"How the hell is my dad marrying a woman other than my mom? But maybe Lena is not my mom at all."

"So, is Dad my father?"

"Okay, stop, Frank. Stop thinking, and just get information that might lead to the answers."

I suddenly felt like an orphaned little boy, unsure of his place in the world without the story behind how he got there. How can you move toward your future if your past is so screwed up? How can you figure out the world when you don't know your place in it?

My parents—or the people I'd always known to be Ma and Dad—had always been good to me. They'd given me a nice, typical childhood. I'd always had all I needed, even when times were tight with their finances. I'd thought as a kid that Dad must be doing well if Ma came home with a new dress or hairdo. One day, when I was young, and after Dad got home from work, Ma excitedly came down the stairs and twirled into the kitchen for Dad. "What d'ya think?" she'd asked with a proud grin as she modeled her new spring dress. But Dad barely glanced at her as he looked through the mail on the counter. Ma's shoulders slumped. I knew I had to do something. "You look like a beautiful princess, Ma!" I'd offered, quick to not allow the smile to fade from her face.

There had been countless times like that in our house. Another time, Ma had spent weeks scouring magazines for just the right new hairdo to try. She'd torn out photos and tucked them into her handbag so she could speak with her stylist at the local beauty parlor. I had been in the fifth grade, but even still, I remembered as I walked home from school that day that Ma had gone to get her hair done. When I walked into our house through the back door like always, Ma was using her hand mixer. She looked sad, even more so than usual. I'd seen Dad's truck outside, so I knew he was home early. That had to be it, I realized.

"Ma! Your hair looks amazing!" I grinned as I put my books down.

My mom kept mixing as she forced a tight-lipped smile but didn't look directly at me. I was sure then. Dad hadn't noticed her hairdo.

"Seriously, Ma," I added. "You look just like the movie stars in your magazines!"

"Thanks, Frank," Ma said, with tears in her eyes.

Dad was in the living room, but I didn't speak to him. Instead, I stomped upstairs and went to my room. I would've slammed my door, but I knew not to if I didn't want trouble. It was another unspoken thing in our neighborhood. People worked hard for what they had, and they demanded it be respected. My friends and I knew the rules were interchangeable between our households. And if any one of us should step out of line, our mothers were interchangeable, too. It was unspoken, but any mother could discipline any other mother's child if he got out of line, so long as his own mother wasn't there to do it herself.

As I sat in my parents' basement, surrounded by ghosts of the past, I wondered if it had been my own mother who'd washed my mouth out with soap when I'd tried the f-word one day, just to be like the men I'd heard working with Dad. I wondered if it had been my real mom who'd smacked the backs of my thighs with a rolled newspaper when she heard I'd been fighting. Had it been my real mom who'd nursed me through chickenpox? Or held my hand while the doctor stitched my knee after I'd crashed my bike? Had it been my real mom who'd hugged me after my first breakup with a girl? Who was the woman upstairs who'd always put others before herself, and who'd tried for so long to turn her husband's head?

I read another letter, and then another one:

Miles may separate us right now, Johnny, but soon, we'll be able to be together every minute for the rest of our lives.

I'll be proud to call you my husband, and being your wife is all I've ever wanted.

Almost all the letters were signed similarly: Eternally yours or Eternally, Rose.

Whoever this Rose woman was, she'd clearly been head over heels in love with Johnny, my dad, or the man I'd thought to be my dad. Potential scenarios ricocheted in my head. Decades had obviously passed since the photos were taken, and yet, no one had ever mentioned the bizarre story behind them. Worse still, who was the dark-haired beauty in the pictures?

There were more newspaper clippings. One read, *BRIDE BURIED AT TEARFUL RITE.* Another said, *BRIDE DIES AT HER WEDDING.* One photo showed the bride beside her father. The caption read, *On her father's arm, the bride starts up the steps to the church.* I stared in confusion at the picture and realized the tuxedoed man beside the bride was a much younger Papa D. It was Vito DeFabrizio. "I gave her my arm, my beautiful little girl," the bride's father had commented in the article.

I'd heard hushed rumblings as a kid, something about Mama D and Papa Vito losing a daughter a long time ago. But no one ever talked about it around the DeFabrizios, almost as if it were a taboo subject. Even as a kid, I'd somehow known to avoid talking about their daughter, like everyone else did. I'd presumed they'd lost their daughter when she'd been a young girl, but the photos depicted a grown woman.

It was getting late. I'd been sitting on the workshop floor for nearly two hours, but the more I read, the more confused I felt. Worse still, I knew no one would give me answers, since no one ever talked about whatever I had uncovered. If they hadn't spoken of it for decades, I felt sure no one would want to talk about the story behind the photos and articles. I carefully replaced all the old letters and placed the lock of hair atop the rubber-banded stack. Before I shut the lid of the footlocker, I stared again at a photo of a much younger Johnny. His relaxed face was happy. Even his eyes smiled as he stood beside the pretty girl in the picture. But the girl was not Ma, and I'd never seen Dad look as contented and happy as he did in that old photo. It was like the young, uniformed soldier in the picture was a different person than the Johnny I'd always known as my father. My dad's eyes now looked tired, pained, and hollow, as if they'd seen too much over time. I shook my head and wondered when he had lost that glint in his eye that made him look like he was on top of world.

I slid the footlocker back into its place on the bottom shelf and replaced the old tarp where I'd found it, covering the top of the box. Then, clueless about what to do next, I switched off the light and then shut the workshop door, once again entombing secrets of the past. As I left my parents' home, I wondered about the people who slept upstairs, the ones I'd known my whole life but apparently hadn't known well at all.

I walked next door to my house, but as I slid my key in my front door, I thought better of it. Why go into my empty house when Debbie wasn't inside and waiting for me? I'd only lie in bed and stare at the ceiling anyway. So, I turned and got into my truck in the driveway. The streets were quiet as I drove through town. Most people were tucked away for the night and preparing for the predictable day that was to come.

"Yeah. You can all sleep. You know who you are, who your families are, and everything there is to know about where you came from," I thought.

If I couldn't sleep before, I'd never sleep now, not with the mysterious discovery I'd just made. Without thinking about it, I parked outside the Den, a small bar in town that time had forgotten. People said nothing had changed inside the bar in decades, not even the framed photos that had hung on the walls since locals had last gone off to war. I'd been going into the bar since before I was old enough to be in there.

"Little late for you on a weeknight, Frank," the bartender said as he put a beer in front of me.

"Hey, Brian," I nodded. "Thanks."

He could tell I didn't feel like talking. Brian was like his dad, the bar's original owner. He spoke to his patrons if they wanted to talk, but he could tell when people wanted to be left to their thoughts, too. He read me perfectly as I leaned on the bar, lost in my thoughts, and drank my beer. Brian walked away to go and dry some glasses, careful to rub off even the slightest water spots like his dad had taught him as a kid. I'd known Brian for years. But now, I envied him that he knew about his family and that he'd sleep that night.

"Aye, Brian, another one?" I said as I raised my empty glass.

"You got it, Frank."

I tipped back my glass and emptied it in three big chugs, trying to rinse away the ache in my chest. Then, before I could ask for another one, Brian slid one to me from down the bar.

"Woman troubles?" Brian asked.

"You could say that."

When my beer was almost gone, I carried my glass over to the piano that had stood in the bar for decades. Since it was a weeknight, there weren't many people in the bar, and it was quiet. I set my glass on the edge of the piano and then sat down on the piano bench. I'd played some piano since I was a kid, and I had a few favorite songs, but my fingers had a mind of their own, I guess. Surrounded by framed vintage photos of WWII GI's, I began to play "More Than You Know," the song Dad had always hummed that was on the record I had found in the workshop.

My fingers moved across the piano keys with an aggressive vigor I had never known. The silent men in the photos stared unflinchingly, their war stories lost forever and now unspoken, just like those in the photos in my parents' basement. As I played the song, I stared down the photos across from the piano like they were my enemies. The men in them were wearing the same uniform Johnny, my dad, the stranger, had in the newspaper photos.

The big-haired, flirty cocktail waitress walked over and placed a fresh beer in front of me.

"Hey, Sharon. Thanks," I said as I kept playing.

She slid beside me on the piano bench to make sure I got a good view of her ample cleavage that was barely contained in her low-cut top.

"How ya doin', Frank?" she asked.

"Wish I knew. Seems like everything in my world is

unraveling, and there's nothing I can do but just sit and watch it happen." I shook my head.

CHAPTER 8

"Ayyy! What the," Dad yelled as I squinted at the offending sunlight and tried to shield my eyes with my arm as I sat up in my front seat. My body ached, but my head hurt worse still.

Dad jerked open the passenger door of my truck. As I looked around groggily, I saw I'd done a poor job of parking just before dawn and had missed my driveway by half a yard. I don't mean half a yard, like eighteen inches. I mean I'd parked on Dad's lawn instead of in my yard.

"Look what ya done here, Frank! C'mon! Tire treads tearin' up my grass! You're gonna fix all this shit!"

Before I could completely process whatever he'd said, my dad reached in, yanked my keys out of the ignition, and grabbed my half-empty bottle.

"Hey! That's Kentucky friggin' Bluegrass!" I objected.

"Yeah? And it stinks like a damned distillery-turned-flophouse in here! Now go take a shower before ya mother sees you like this. I'll move the truck—if I can hold my breath long enough to get it off my lawn that you're killin' here!"

Begrudgingly, I peeled myself from my truck's passenger seat, which I'd literally stuck to it with stale, sticky whiskey. As I stood up, I struggled to maintain balance as my torso righted itself. Dad shook his head.

"What the hell's wrong with you?" he asked.

I glared at him and tried to focus on the man I'd thought was my father, one of the people I trusted most in the world.

"What are ya lookin' at?" Dad spat.

"I got *no* idea," I said honestly. "None."

*

Later that afternoon, after I'd showered and slept some, I walked next door. I had to admit that the tire tracks had torn up Dad's lawn, all right. It would have to wait until tomorrow, though, until my head quit throbbing.

"Hey," I said as I shuffled in the back door to find Ma, Dad, and Aunt Gina playing cards and drinking wine from juice glasses, as they'd done all my life.

"Finally!" Ma said. "Bobby called first thing, and I told a little white lie. I said you were sick."

"Doesn't look like a lie to me." Aunt Gina laughed as she sized me up. "You get the numba of the bus that hit ya?"

"Nah, it backed up and ran me over again, too."

I flopped into a nearby upholstered chair and watched the three of them in the home that had been the only family home I'd known. But who were these people?

Dad crossed his arms and eyed me with a cold stare, as if challenging me to say or do something.

"What the hell you lookin' at?" I said to him.

"Frankie! Ma said.

There it was again—*Frankie*—so I know she meant business, but I ignored her and stared back at my dad.

"You know," I said, "you really oughta clean out the basement. It's filled with a bunch of old shit you don't need anymore."

"Frank!" Ma defended him. "What're you talkin' about? That's your *father's* junk."

"No, let him talk. What're you getting at, Frank?" Dad said without taking his eyes off me.

"C'mon. Play your cards already, will ya?" Aunt Gina told her brother. "Can't you see he's still drunk?"

"What do *you* think I'm gettin' at?" I tauntingly asked him as I returned his piercing stare.

"Okay! That's enough!" Gina said as she threw her hand of cards onto the table. "We've all had too much, it seems. C'mon, Frank. Walk me home?"

Aunt Gina pushed back her chair, and it screeched across the linoleum floor. But I didn't move, so she came closer, put a firm hand on my shoulder, and squeezed.

"Walk me home, Frank," she repeated with more emphasis.

"Whatever," I finally said as I got up gave Dad one final hard stare.

The air was thick and heavy. Ma said nothing as Gina held open the back door for me. Both women sensed that things could get physical. They both knew Gina needed to separate Dad and me, and quick. I'd never wanted to hit my father, but with all the rage built up inside me, I wasn't sure I could contain it. Dad looked like he felt the same, as he eyed me walking outside with Aunt Gina.

Aunt Gina's shoulders relaxed when we got outside, but I struggled to calm myself. My head throbbed, and the daylight pierced my skin like a million daggers as Gina and I walked down the driveway toward the street. She lived a few doors down.

"Hey, the Garavusos' house is goin' up for sale," she said. "After three generations."

I said nothing about my aunt's attempt to change the topic and distract me. But she went on. "And I never thought I'd miss the DiMartellis, but, you know—"

"Yeah? And what about the DeFabrizios?" I interrupted.

Aunt Gina stopped walking and stood in the spot where my words had dropped on her like a house. I stared at her, looking for a reaction. She shut her eyes, sighed, and then took my arm, and we started walking toward her house again.

"So, you know," she said.

But she'd said it in the affirmative, as a statement of fact, not as a question. So, there was indeed *something* to know. But I didn't want to admit that I didn't know all of it, or the crucial parts, anyway.

"You tell *me*," I urged, desperate to know more as my aunt and I played a cautious cat-and-mouse game.

Gina sighed deeply. "What more can I say, Frank? It was a terrible, terrible thing, and we all agreed it's best to leave it all behind us. In fact, your mother was the one who insisted on it. It was the only way she'd marry your father."

I stopped walking and stared at her as she held my arm.

"So, please. *Please*, just leave the basement alone."

"You know," I began as I cocked my head, "I would if *he* would. But he's down there spending time with her just about every damn night!"

"What? What d'ya mean?" Gina looked shocked as she tried to imagine how that could be. "That's not possible, Frank. They made a deal. That can't be!"

"Well, there's a footlocker down there in the basement that says you're wrong. No wonder Ma could never get Dad to go to church. He's got a friggin' shrine down there. So why go to church?" I spat with disgust.

"That dumb bastard," Gina said as she shook her head in disbelief.

We walked in silence along the edge of the same street where I'd grown up and past the neighbor's driveway where I'd once crashed my bike. We walked beneath the same streetlights that had come on for years, signaling that all the neighborhood kids needed to be home. It was a street I knew well—or that I thought I'd known well. But was any of it real? Had my life been real if my parents weren't who I'd thought they were, and if Dad had held onto some deeply ingrained love for the woman in the newspaper clippings?

Finally, I said, "So, what'd she die of? Rose. What killed her?"

Gina just shrugged without looking at me. "She died, Frank. Back then, sometimes people just died unexpectedly. You know?"

"What? Seriously? You don't know?" I asked. "No one even bothered to find out what killed her?"

"Guess not." Gina shrugged again. "It was a long time ago, Frank. Times were different back then. We just accepted it, I guess."

"So, you're tellin' me that your future sister-in-law suddenly dropped dead on her wedding day, and no one cared enough to find out what happened?"

"You gotta understand, Frankie. We'd dealt with a lot of tragedy in our family before Rose's death. Your father and I had lost both of our parents, and our sister, all in the span of about two years before this happened. We were engulfed in death. So I guess we were numb by that point and just accepted it. She was gone, and there was nothin' we could do that'd bring her back."

"I understand, but she died at the church, for God sake! She was just twenty-one years old! What the hell's wrong with you people?" I asked in shock. "How could no one at least look into it? Not even her own family? Not even Mama or Papa D? You all just accepted it and moved on?"

"Yes, we had no choice but to move on," Gina said again.

"Yeah? Well, I can't. It just doesn't sit well with me."

We stopped in front of Aunt Gina's house. She looked up at me and said, "Frank? C'mon now. I know that look. Don't go and do somethin' stupid. You've got enough problems, trust me."

But I shook off her words and refused to listen to my aunt.

I said. "G'night, Aunt Gina." I gave her a quick peck on the cheek like I'd done for years, even as a kid. She looked worried and concerned when I left her and walked home.

Years earlier, at that time of day, Gina would have started dinner. But her husband, Vinny Napoli, had long since died, and those predictable routines had, too. But though the empty house was still and quiet, Gina wandered to the sideboard covered with dozens of framed photos, many from decades earlier. She picked up the picture of her beloved sister Celia, taken at a fair one day. Celia had looked so happy.

Her genuine smile illuminated the picture as Gina recalled the day it was taken.

✳✳

After a ride on the tilt-a-whirl, Celia had excitedly grabbed Gina's arm and said, "I want popcorn, Gina."

"Oh, sorry, honey. We've been here so long that we've run out of money. So we're going home soon, after a few more rides," Gina told her.

"That's not fair! Vinny had three hot dogs!" Celia protested.

"Aw, for the love of," Vinny said as he rolled his eyes.

But Kevin, a friend of Vinny's and Gina's, cut in and said, "Come on, Celia. I'll get you the best popcorn on the midway!"

"Is it okay, Gina? Can I go with Kevin for popcorn? Can I?" Celia asked with the innocence of a young girl.

"Yeah, just don't drown it in butter again." Gina laughed.

"Good riddance," Vinny mumbled under his breath.

Celia saluted her sister as Gina adjusted her oversize embroidered shawl.

"Today, Gina, today," Vinny complained when Gina fawned over Celia.

Kevin squinted and stared in disgust at Vinny's selfishness, yet Vinny couldn't have cared less. He'd always seen Celia as a third wheel he'd had to tolerate so he could date Gina.

"Come on!" Kevin winked at Celia. "How 'bout if we

drown the popcorn just a little with butter?"

With a skip in her step, twenty-four-year-old Celia ran off with Kevin, thrilled that her sister's friends were always so nice to her.

"Why do you have to be so mean?" Gina spun around and asked Vinny.

"Aw, come on! Enough is enough! She's always around, Gina! She's attached at your hip!"

"Yeah? So, what's gonna happen when she comes to live with us one day? What then, Vinny?"

"When?" Vinny repeated as he shut his eyes and shook his head. "Don't you mean *if* she comes to live with us one day?"

Gina shot him a look that told him he'd be better off if he just shut up. Vinny never did know how to read the room or when to drop something, so he persisted.

"Look, I signed on to you, not your sister and definitely not Captain America!" Vinny spat.

"So, now you've got a problem with *Johnny*, too?"

But before Vinny could answer, Johnny stepped out of the crowd. "Who's got a problem with Johnny?" Johnny asked.

"Me! Where the hell you been, man?" Vinny asked him.

But before he replied, Rose stepped closer to Johnny and took his hand. "My fault! Sorry." She smiled.

"Rose, this is my buddy, Vinny Napoli, and my sister Gina," Johnny told Rose.

"And this is Rose DeFabrizio. Just moved out here from

Rosedale," Johnny told Vinny and Gina.

"Hey, Rosie from Rosedale," Vinny said as he extended his hand, already smitten with the beautiful girl Johnny had just introduced.

But Gina saw Vinny's reaction to Rose, and she moved in to take control of the situation. "Hi," she said as she shook her hand. "Nice to meet you, Rose. Johnny's told us nothing about you—which is kinda strange since it seems like you two are pretty chummy."

Johnny didn't address his sister's comment, although he knew Gina was surprised by Rose. But Johnny had preferred to lay low and fly under the radar until he was ready to share his girl with the world.

"So much goin' on in the world now, right? Who keeps track of it all? Hey, where's Celia?" he asked as he protectively looked around for his sister, as he'd done his whole life.

"Oh, Celia is with Kevin, the patron saint of third wheeling," Vinny scoffed as he rolled his eyes. "She's fine. She's always fine. How could she *not* be, with an army of people always watchin' out for her? You guys will definitely be ready for children, after all these years of takin' care of Celia. But who will find time to make babies when you've got her to watch all the time, huh?"

"Come on, you idiot," Gina said as she took Vinny's hand and led him down the midway to find Kevin and Celia.

Johnny was grateful to Gina because he didn't want to dress Vinny down in front of Rose. The group made their way through the crowd, said hello to a few people they knew, and finally found Kevin and Celia near a big, colorful popcorn cart. Celia was happily licking butter from her fingertips.

"Hey, let's go to the Ferris wheel next," Johnny said to Celia, just to watch her face light up. He loved to see his older sister happy. When her face lit up, all was right with the world, and their whole family felt the same way.

"Yaaaay! The Ferris wheel! Yesssss!" Celia squealed with a mouthful of popcorn.

"But first, I want you to meet someone," Johnny told her. "This is Rose."

"Hi, Celia. Nice to meet you," Rose smiled as she took Celia's hand and shook it, just like she would anyone else's.

Celia loved when people treated her like a grown up, and handshakes were an adult sort of greeting to her. Rose was like most of Johnny and Gina's friends. They treated Celia with respect and looked after her like one of their own younger siblings.

"Can you get into a bucket on the Ferris wheel, Celia, with those greasy fingertips, I mean?" Johnny laughed.

"They're not buttery now, Johnny!" Celia proudly showed him as she held up five fingers that she'd just licked clean. "And can I ride with you, Johnny? You know I get a little scared sometimes."

The group of six made their way toward the huge, lit-up Ferris wheel at the end of the midway. Music played all around as lights of all colors illuminated the fairground. Carnies tried to wave the group over to play games or purchase souvenirs and snacks, but Johnny politely smiled and waved them all off.

"Um, you guys, I think I'll sit this one out," Vinny said. "You know, my thing about heights and all."

"Suit yourself," Gina said as she continued with the group while Vinny took a seat on a nearby bench.

Not even ten minutes later, a carnival worker held a metal bar open so Celia, Rose, Johnny, Gina, and Kevin could step into a Ferris wheel bucket. "Hands and feet inside the ride at all times," the worker said in a monotone that suggested he'd prefer to be anyplace other than at work that night.

Celia became noticeably anxious when the bar locked in place, and the worker went to the next bucket to let Gina and Kevin get in. Johnny wrapped his arm around Celia's shoulder, since she suddenly seemed uncertain about the ride. Everyone had noticed, even Kevin, who had had been staring at Gina since taking his seat.

"I'm so happy to meet you, Celia, *finally*," Rose said. "Johnny has told me all about you."

"Oh, no. Like what? What'd Johnny tell you?" Celia asked, wide-eyed.

"I've heard nothing but great things about you!" Rose laughed as she gently touched Celia's embroidered shawl. "This is beautiful. I'll bet you made it, didn't you, Celia?"

Celia proudly nodded. "I'm teaching Gina now, too!"

"Wow! You're a talented artist and a teacher! I hear that you're sweet on Mickey Rooney, too. Is that right?"

Celia looked embarrassed as her cheeks turned bright pink. "Am not," she said. "Besides, he'd never look at me."

"Well now, that'd be his loss," Rose told her new friend.

"Definitely!" Kevin agreed, just as the Ferris wheel suddenly lurched.

"Ohhhh!" Celia gasped as she put a hand on her stomach, but the wheel moved again, and this time, it kept going.

As if a switch had suddenly flipped, Celia reached under her big shawl and pulled out a brown glass medicine bottle from her dress pocket. She took a pre-measured sip and then replaced the cap on the bottle.

"What's that for?" Rose asked her.

"Nerves. I get nerves," Celia said.

As the Ferris wheel music played, Rose opened her purse and pulled out a pink bottle that she held up to Celia. "See? We all need something at one time or another. I need this pink stuff when my stomach doesn't feel good, too."

"Yours is a prettier color than mine!" Celia smiled. "I like pink!"

Rose raised her pink bottle and clinked it with Celia's

brown medicine bottle. "Cheers! Here's to us girls and our nerves!"

Celia loved that Rose treated her like an adult, just like one of the others. Celia knew she was different, but everyone had always told her it was just because she was so unique and precious that she felt unlike everyone else. Most times, Celia believed it and focused on sharing her kindness and making people smile. Like clockwork, her neighbors saw Celia sitting outside on her stoop and waving to all the passersby. She loved delivering eggs from her family's chickens to the neighbors or running simple errands for her mother. Whatever Celia did, she did it with a smile, and people loved her for the light she brought into their world.

"You're really nice, Rose," Celia said as she held the hand of her new friend. "And pretty, too. I hope God gives you and Johnny lots of babies when you get married."

"Can I tell you a secret?" Rose leaned in and asked Celia. "I hope so, too."

Kevin shifted uncomfortably as Johnny and Rose's eyes met. Unlike most of the other guys at school, Kevin hadn't been jealous when Johnny had first asked Rose out. It wasn't that he didn't also find Rose attractive, but Kevin had always had eyes for another girl.

As Celia listened to Johnny tell her and Rose about the lights below them in their town, Kevin lowered his voice and said, "I don't get it, Gina. Vinny's a jerk. He treats you like dirt. You deserve so much better."

"What? Like *you*? You knew Johnny's seein' somebody, but you never even mentioned it to me. No, thanks, Kevin. And can you please stop embarrassin' yourself?"

"Embarrassin' myself? *Me*? I'm not the one too afraid to take his girl on a Ferris wheel. Now that's embarrassin', if you ask me. Just sayin'."

"Shut up, Kev." Gina rolled her eyes dramatically and then began scanning the crowd below for Vinny.

"Yeah, your guy's a lotta fun, Gina. Hey, I think that's him down there on that bench talking with those old guys. Looks like they're drinking prune juice and comparing bowel movements. I'd say Vinny fits right in."

"Enough, Kevin!" Gina said, eager to get away from him and his unwanted comments.

"I love you, Gina. Always have and always will," Kevin blurted out.

"Shut up, Kev, or I swear I'll jump."

The ride came to an end, and they all got off the Ferris wheel and walked over to the bench where Vinny sat with two old Italian men, including one who was snoozing with his arms crossed in front of him and an open newspaper over his face.

"That took long enough," Vinny complained as he walked toward them.

"Yeah, the ride was nice. Thanks for askin'," Gina said

sarcastically.

The group started walking up the midway, with Gina, Celia, and Kevin bringing up the rear. Rose and Johnny held hands as they talked with Vinny. Suddenly, Vinny veered to the right, without a second thought about Gina or what she wanted to do. He pointed up ahead to something, and Johnny and Rose followed his lead.

"C'mon now. What's up with that?" Kevin scoffed as he flipped his hand toward Vinny. "Gina, you gotta admit it's real classy how Vinny just ignored you and took off with Johnny, like you're not even here," he scoffed. "Guess I should thank him for that, huh?"

Gina didn't answer. Kevin was relentless, and he always had been. They stopped talking when they arrived at the shooting gallery where Johnny and Vinny were engaged in a competitive shootout as Rose looked on.

POP! POP! POP! POP! POP-POP-POP!

Johnny and Vinny fired off rounds that tore holes through the paper stars in the back of the shooting gallery as the attendant watched. But Vinny seemed to be aggressively firing his gun, as if engaged in a real shootout.

"That's some girl you got there. When you gonna introduce her to Lena?" Vinny asked Johnny.

"Eh, it's not like that."

"Yeah? Well, somebody better tell Lena Aschettino that, huh?" Vinny asked as he squeezed off a few more rounds.

POP! POP! POP!

"Take that, Hitler!" Vinny said.

POP! POP! POP! POP!

"Choke on it, Mussolini! You make me ashamed to be Italian!"

POP! POP! POP!

"Why don't you go and fight?" Johnny asked.

"Eh, busted eardrum, you know?" Vinny shrugged. "How 'bout you? Why don't you go?"

"Oh, I'm goin'. Soon as I turn eighteen," Johnny said proudly.

POP! POP! POP! POP-POP!

Vinny took out the last of his stars and said, "The way you shoot? You'll come home in a soup can, man!"

"I'll take my chances," Johnny said.

"What about Celia? You can't just leave her with Gina."

"She'll be good. I'm more worried about leavin' Rose." Johnny sighed.

After Vinny had shot out all his stars, he relaxed and seemed suddenly satisfied and happy, waiting for Johnny to finish shooting out his own. He put a hand on Johnny's shoulder and said, "It'll be okay, pal. But you go and hit Hitler where he lives! Don't worry about a thing here in Inwood."

*

"So long ago," Gina said to herself as she replaced the framed photo of her beloved sister Celia, who'd passed away years earlier. She just hoped Frank would leave it alone and not dredge up old ghosts. Everyone was better off if they didn't bring it up again—any of it.

CHAPTER 9

A few days after I talked with Aunt Gina, I knew I couldn't take it any longer. I grabbed my keys, jumped in my truck, and headed toward the downtown government offices and the courthouse. Somebody had to know something. A death certificate had to exist, and since someone had unexpectedly died, and at a young age, there had to be a coroner's report of some kind. Although decades had passed, I figured the town must have investigated sudden deaths, even back then.

I whipped my pickup into the first open parking spot and jumped out. A large American flag whipped in the wind overhead as I went inside the old, musty-smelling office building. Everywhere I looked was a monochromatic grayish pallor. The walls, the desks, the floors, the people—they all blended together in the most uneventful way inside the building, where time seemed to have stood still. The building even smelled old, sort of like a library had merged with a forgotten, dank dungeon.

"Help you, sir?" the disinterested, gum-popping woman asked from behind her glass partition. I was paralyzed with disbelief as I noticed she wore a gray cardigan over a dull, beige blouse, atop taupe slacks, and she even wore beige-rimmed eyeglasses and had tan-painted fingernails. She blended in with the decor as if she'd been there for as long as the oldest files. I imagined that she never left and only existed behind that glass partition, never seeing sunlight or blue sky because she didn't know anything existed beyond the gray walls around her.

"Sir?" she repeated.

"Oh, yeah, sorry." I shook myself from my thoughts. "I'm looking for medical records or a coroner's report on a death from the 1940s."

"You're kiddin', right?" she asked as she lowered her head to look at me over her beige eyeglasses.

"No, ma'am. I'm serious."

"Well, we've put some of that old stuff on hard drives. Years ago, some records were transferred to microfilm. We lost some files when the archive room flooded after the pipes froze and burst one year," the clerk said. "That was a long time ago, though."

"I know, but it's important. Can you help me?" I asked.

She picked up a nearby clipboard and pushed it across her counter to me. "Fill this out," she curtly responded, "and we'll see what we've got. But no promises."

I took the clipboard, grabbed a flower-tipped pen from the cup on the counter, and stepped aside to fill out the government form that had been photocopied so many times it was almost illegible in places. Then, when I'd finished, I walked back to the woman and handed her the clipboard.

"Oh," she said as she wrinkled her nose. "It's 1946? I see. Have a seat and gimme a few minutes, okay?"

I slipped quarters into a nearby vending machine and got a soda for myself before I went to sit in the nearby waiting area. There were some recent copies of *Life* magazine displayed in a fan shape on the end table. I picked up a copy of *Newsday* and anxiously thumbed through it. I couldn't settle down, and my shaking knee had a mind of its own. Time moved slowly as I waited for anything that might bring answers about what had happened to the pretty bride forever memorialized in my dad's basement.

"Mister Mastantuono?" the clerk called from behind her glass partition.

I rocketed to my feet and catapulted to her counter, unwilling to wait for even a second longer to find out about the young woman whose memory was still a part of my father. The clerk removed her glasses as she held up an old, thin file folder.

"Great! You found the file!" I exclaimed, sure that my answers were within my reach.

But the clerk let the folder drop open, and it was empty. My heart sank.

"Well, I found the file," she said. "But it's empty. Not a single note, record, or photograph in it. I'm sorry. I've never had this happen before; that's quite odd. Maybe when they moved things around, or when we began to transfer those old paper records to digital files, the contents got misfiled or lost."

"Just my luck." I shook my head. "What was I thinkin' anyway? Somethin' that old and all. Thanks for tryin'."

I walked outside and under the stars and stripes that flew proudly over the building. Something just didn't feel right in my gut. But I wasn't sure where to turn next or what to do. I drove toward my house as all the same questions pummeled me, one after another, joined by a few new ones now.

As soon as I'd turned into my driveway, Dad flew out his front door and stomped across his yard toward mine. I'd only seen that expression a few times, and none of those times had ended well. My dad was still a solid guy. He kept in shape through his physical work. Most preferred to steer clear of Johnny when his nostrils flared and his jaws tightened.

"Ay! I wanna talk to you!" Dad yelled through my truck's open passenger window.

I got out and slammed my door and rounded the hood of my truck to stand in front and look him in the eye.

"Good, 'cause I wanna talk to you, too!" I yelled. "And I want Ma to hear!"

But as I took a step to walk past him and toward his yard, he stepped in front of me to stop me from passing.

"What the hell do you think you're doin'?" he asked.

"Lookin' for answers."

"It don't concern you, Frank!"

"You got some set a stones tellin' me that!" I yelled.

"Look." Dad sighed. "Things were just different back then, that's all. People just—"

"People just *died*. Yeah, I heard all that. So, how come they never closed the case, then? Tell me that! If people just died, dropped dead away, and if that was so common, then why wasn't the case ever closed?"

"How do you know that?" Dad asked with a glint of surprise in his eye.

"Are you serious? Twenty-year-old girls don't just drop dead, and how many girls drop dead on their wedding days? Does that make sense to you?" I yelled.

"Well, I dunno," he said. "But that's what happened."

"I need a beer," I said as I turned to go toward my front door. Dad followed me inside my house.

I tossed my keys in one motion, and they slid across the kitchen counter as I yanked open the refrigerator. I left the door open as I opened the bottle with the opener I kept on my counter. Dad reached in and helped himself to a beer, too, and then shut the refrigerator. He opened his beer, and we both tipped back our bottles and eyed each other as we gulped and swallowed. Tension hung between us as the oxygen was sucked out of the room.

Finally, Dad took his bottle from his lips and asked, "So, what'd you find out?"

"Nothin' but another dead end. I should be used to it by now." I shook my head.

"Dead end? What d'ya mean by dead end, Frank?"

"The file's gone, just disappeared—or at least, the *contents* of the file are gone. No notes. No record of who took the reports from the file. Nothin'. How 'bout that?" I asked sarcastically.

Dad stared blankly into space as he took a long, angry swig of beer. But then, his face changed. He looked as if he'd put together something in his mind, as if something had finally clicked for him. I said nothing as I waited for him to tell me what he'd just thought.

"Look! What do you want me to say?" he asked. "I was gonna have one life, but it didn't work out. So, I didn't cry about it. I just moved on, that's all."

"No, you *didn't*, Dad!" I yelled.

My dad stepped back, as if my words had slammed into him and knocked him off his balance. The realization that I was right hit him like a freight train.

"Listen! You either tell Ma about the footlocker, or I will," I threatened.

"What's wrong with you? You wanna hurt your mother for no damned good reason, then you go right ahead," Johnny challenged.

"*You're* the one who's hurting Ma! It's been goin' on for years! She deserves to know why! Don't you think?" With that, I slammed my empty bottle down on the countertop.

"Well, don't think for a second this is gonna fix your screwed-up life, not for a second! You're only makin' things worse!" Dad yelled.

"Tell her, Dad! You, tell her, or I will!"

"You're an asshole!" he hollered.

"Yeah? Like father, like son."

Johnny guzzled the rest of his beer down and then slammed his bottle on the counter and stormed out of the house. He sensed that his whole existence was about to implode and rain down collateral damage everywhere. As he stomped across his lawn, Johnny glared contemptuously at the deep tire tracks in his grass that Frank had yet to repair. He cursed his son under his breath for disturbing the order of his household, both literally and figuratively.

*

When Johnny walked in his back door, Lena wasn't around. The kitchen smelled of fresh bread, so Johnny went over and cut a piece off the loaf cooling on the counter. He presumed Lena was upstairs, either reading or maybe putting away some laundry, so Johnny went to lie down on his couch and think about what to do.

An hour later, without a peep from Lena, Johnny wondered if she was upstairs at all. He got up and climbed the stairs two at a time until he reached the top landing. The upstairs was neat as a pin, but there was no sign of his wife.

"Lena?" Johnny called as he went to check their bathroom for her. "You up here, Lena?"

She hadn't been outside in the yard, she wasn't upstairs, and it didn't seem like she was even inside the house. But panic suddenly gripped Johnny, and he pivoted and rushed out of their bedroom and down the stairs. When he got to the kitchen, he stopped and stared at the basement door.

"No," he thought. "She never goes down there, not ever."

With a shaky hand, he reached for the metal doorknob and turned it slowly. The light was already on when he opened the door. Johnny's heart started to beat faster. Sweat beaded on his brow and upper lip as a sick feeling settled in his gut. Slowly, he walked down the wooden steps as if walking toward the guillotine. When he saw the light coming from his workshop, Johnny felt like he might pass out.

Emotions clashed within him as he realized someone had dared intrude on his privacy. That workshop was meant for Rose and him, a place to relive their memories and reconnect.

His wife did not belong on the other side of that door. Johnny felt violated and disrespected, but he knew it would be much worse than that.

He stood silently in the doorway and looked at all his memories laid out on the floor at Lena's feet. She looked up from where she stood, holding fistfuls of newspaper clippings and old photos. As she stared at Johnny, angry, hot tears filled her eyes and then fell on her already tear-stained cheeks.

"How could you?" she asked as she shook her head. "It's bad enough that I've spent my whole life bein' second best, nothin' more than some worthless consolation prize that you'd had to settle on. But this? Every night, John. This is what you're doin' down here? How could you?"

There was nothing he could say. The jig was up, and nothing Johnny could say would make his wife feel any better. He helplessly turned his palms toward the ceiling and shrugged. "What d'ya want me to say?"

Lena threw the handfuls of pictures and articles at him, but one picture stuck to her palm. "No ghosts! We agreed, John! No ghosts!" As Lena shook the photo of Rose from her hand, she slapped at it with her other hand, and it ripped in half.

"Leave her alone! You leave her *alone*!" Johnny screamed as he grabbed

Lena's wrists hard and glared down at her.

The look in Johnny's eyes sickened her. Lena felt betrayed and unimportant to the man to whom her life was devoted. She thought she might throw up as she and Johnny stared long and hard at each other with Johnny's memories scattered all around them.

Finally, Lena pulled and tried to free herself from Johnny's firm grip. Johnny opened his hands and let her go. Lena brushed past him, stepping on letters and photos as she left the workshop and then marched upstairs. She made a beeline to their master bedroom, opened her closet, jerked a suitcase from a shelf, and threw it on her bed. With little thought about what to pack—much less of where to go—Lena pulled clothes from her closet, folded them, and filled the suitcase with all it could hold. She grabbed her makeup bag and toiletries and crammed them into the bulging suitcase. Fueled by fury, Lena zipped and buckled the suitcase closed, hefted it off her bed, and haphazardly got it down the stairs as she fought her swinging handbag that hung on her shoulder.

There was no sign of John. Lena knew he was still down in the basement, still cloistered away with the memories of the girl he'd always loved. She stopped to grab her coat from the front closet, along with a scarf that she tied around her head and knotted under her chin. As she lugged the heavy suitcase out her front door, Lena realized she wasn't sure where to go. But she knew she couldn't stay in that house another minute with John. It was too crowded with Rose there, and Lena felt like she couldn't breathe as John's memories smothered them.

Lena stood on her front porch, ready to embark on her future if only she knew where to go. Finally, she hoisted her bulging suitcase and lugged it across her lawn, past the tire tracks in the grass, and next door to Frank's house.

She knocked on his front door and then waited. Lena heard Frank's footsteps coming down the stairs. When he pulled open his door, Frank frowned. He knew it had somehow been his fault that his mom had packed up and left his dad. Without a word, he reached for his mom's suitcase and held the door open for Lena to enter.

"Let me go and put sheets on the other bed, Ma," Frank said.

"Oh, I can do it. Don't worry about it. What else am I good for if not handling laundry and makin' beds, right? I've had decades to do nothing but take care of the house and your father. No, I'll do it, Frank. Just leave it."

He shut the door.

CHAPTER 10

The next day came, but Johnny didn't leave his house, and Lena stayed inside Frank's home, next door. Finally, out of exasperation, Johnny got in his truck that evening and went for a drive around town. When he came to Willow Tavern, the same pub Frank had gone to when he'd needed to blow off some steam, Johnny pulled into the parking lot. He just sat in his truck and stared at the door to the tavern, which hadn't changed at all over the years. He watched as men and women came and went, and thought back to one night when he'd been there in 1944.

**

Dressed in his Army uniform, he'd sauntered around the pool table inside, lined up his shot, and taken it. The three ball hung menacingly at a pocket's lip, right at the edge, as the onlookers collectively sighed. Johnny dropped his head in apparent defeat. Behind him, Vinny and Kevin did the same.

Augie Dunbar, thirtyish and cocky, puffed out his chest—nearly as far as his belly protruded—and said, "Tough luck, kid. You wanna double it up midstream?"

"Nah, he don't," Vinny jumped in.

"Ha! Double it up yours!" Johnny challenged Augie. "How 'bout *triple*?"

Kevin and Vinny rolled their eyes in unison as Augie smirked and then lined up the shot Johnny had left open for him. *WHAP! CLICK-CLACK!* Augie made the shot, but the dying cue ball also nudged Johnny's three ball into the pocket.

"How in the hell?" Augie scratched his head.

Johnny chalked his cue and sized up the table as Augie tried to figure out what had just happened. Then, finally, he leaned down to set up, and he glanced over at Vinny and Kevin and winked as the guys tried not to laugh.

CRACK! WHAP! Colored balls jumped and slammed into pockets on the pool table as Johnny cleared it, and Augie scratched his head in confusion.

Rose, Gina, and Celia had been in the tavern that night, too. They sat in a booth in the front room drinking Cokes and leafing through bridal magazines.

"Why's the dress have to be white?" Celia complained. "White is boring."

"Because it just does," Gina said.

But her answer didn't satisfy Celia's curiosity, so Rose gave it a try.

"White is traditional, Celia," Rose explained. "Traditions endure for all time, just like marriages and love endure over time. Wearing white is like making a statement that the bride and groom will be together for all eternity."

"Oh! Now I get it. That sounds nice. You'll be a beautiful bride, Rose!" Celia beamed. "I can't wait to be at your wedding to Johnny! And we'll be like sisters, just like Gina and I are, after you get married!"

"Yes, we will." Rose smiled. "And I can't wait!"

"Me either," Celia agreed as she sipped Coca-Cola through a paper straw.

Suddenly, the tavern's front door opened. Lena Aschettino came in, along with three girlfriends. Lena surveyed the pub as her friends stood slightly behind her waiting for a cue to move. Johnny played pool in the backroom as his sisters and Rose laughed while perusing through bridal magazines. Lena walked closer to their booth and saw the glamorous bridal photos atop the table.

"I love this one!" Rose gushed. "Look at the sweetheart neckline and the way the fabric cascades from the waist!"

"You'd look so beautiful in that!" Celia confirmed.

Lena snickered and rolled her eyes in the girls' direction. She then slid into a booth near the front door, careful to turn her back to Rose, the one girl who stood in the way of Lena getting to Johnny.

"You get any dress you want," Johnny said as he walked up to Rose's booth and slapped down a wad of cash on the table in front of her. "Nothin' is too good for you."

"My hero!" Rose laughed as Johnny slid into the booth beside her and then kissed her on the lips.

Johnny then looked across at Gina and Celia. "You two help her out while I'm gone, and I don't just mean with the dress."

"You got it, bro. Just come home safe, okay?" Gina said as she touched her brother's hand on the tabletop.

"He better!" Celia added. "Johnny better come home safe!"

"Yes, ma'am. Will do." Johnny laughed as he saluted Celia.

"And speaking of home," Rose reminded everyone as she looked at her watch.

"Yeah, right." Johnny finished the beer he'd brought over and then placed the glass on the table.

He slid out of the booth and took Rose's hand as she stood up. Gina helped Celia on with her coat, and they headed out as well. Johnny slid his arm around Rose's waist as they walked toward the door. Lena and her friends smiled up at Johnny as he passed, and he nodded at them and forced a smile. As soon as they'd all stepped outside, Johnny suddenly said, "Just a minute. I forgot something. I'll meet you all at the car," and he went back inside the tavern.

As soon as he stepped through the door, Johnny

tentatively approached the table. Lena's friends nudged her to make her get up from their booth and go and talk to him. When Lena stood up, Johnny came closer. She smelled his signature Old Spice cologne, and she melted.

All at once, Johnny and Lena began to speak at the same time. They laughed, and then they did it again.

"Okay, you, first." Lena smiled.

"Oh, I dunno where to start, Lena. Seems like I've known you forever. And I've always liked you. You know that. But not in that way, more as friends. You know what I mean?"

Lena fought to hold back her tears. Finally, unable to speak due to the lump in her throat, she nodded.

"I'm sorry if that sounds—"

"No, don't be silly. Rose is nice. You go ahead. Go and have a good life, John."

Johnny felt bad. He didn't want to hurt her. Lena stood on tiptoe and gently kissed Johnny's cheek as she inhaled his cologne, desperately wanting more, yet resigned that she was not his girl.

She forced a smile and said, "Hey, you should go. They're all waiting for you."

"Take care of yourself, Lena. Good seein' you."

And with that, Lena's hopes for the future dissolved as she watched Johnny walk out the tavern door.

*

Johnny shook off the memory of that night. He turned off

his truck and got out. He leaned back to stretch and then let out a huge sigh as he thought of all that had happened since that night and everything that had led to 2000.

Moments later, Johnny walked into Willow Tavern and saw Kevin McCarthy, now in his seventies and with a shock of white hair that announced his age from a block away. Johnny walked closer and stood by the table. He watched silently as Kevin lined up his shot on the pool table's green felt, never taking his eyes off his intended shot, even as a shadow was cast over the table.

"Hey, you mind?" Kevin said in an irritated tone. But then, he looked up and saw Johnny standing at the end of the table. "What the hell do you want, Johnny?"

"You got somethin' that belongs to me."

"Yeah? Where have I heard that before?" Kevin scoffed as he dropped his cue stick on the pool table and headed toward the tavern's door.

Kevin pushed the door open and rushed outside with Johnny close on his heels. "Get away from me, will ya?" he said to Johnny.

"Her file. You took it, Kevin. I know you did."

Kevin smiled sarcastically and shook his head in disgust. "Man. Over fifty years, and you're still as wrong as ever about everything, Johnny."

But Johnny didn't flinch, nor did he take his eyes off Kevin. Instead, the two men stared at each other with mutual disdain. They'd been friends, but over the years, so much had happened.

"The file," Johnny said. "Bring it to the bench, noon tomorrow. No questions asked. Or else I raise such a stink that you lose your pension from the force for tampering with evidence or whatever the hell you did with those files. It's your call."

Kevin's face hardened, and his lips tightened. He jabbed his fist in the air hard, unable to contain his anger over Johnny's ultimatum.

"That's it! I just forgot I ever knew you!" And with that, Kevin stormed off and got into his car. He gunned the engine and squealed his tires as he peeled out of the parking lot while Johnny watched him go.

*

"I'm going to work, Ma!" Frank called out as he left his house. "Got a big job today!"

"Yeah, okay. See ya tonight."

Minutes later, Lena poked her head out of Frank's front door and looked next door to see if John's truck was gone. Then, satisfied the coast was clear, she walked outside and hurried across the lawn. Lena let herself in her house with her key and then locked the door behind her. Unsure of what she was looking for, Lena eyed her home from a new perspective as her eyes darted to cupboards, drawers, and closets.

She walked into the den that doubled as a home office, sat down at the heavy rolltop desk, and opened it. John usually paid the bills, opened the mail, and handled their finances, so Lena wasn't sure where to start. She randomly sifted through some opened mail, bills that John would pay like clockwork, just as he always did. There were advertising mailers that John had yet to toss and a few notes he'd written to remind himself to shop insurance rates and fertilize the lawn the next time the weatherman called for rain.

Lena leaned back and sighed, uncertain of what she'd hoped to find. Since there was nothing of interest on the desktop, she pulled open the deep drawer by her right knee. Boxes of canceled checks filled the drawer, going back many years. Lena grabbed a box and went through it, one canceled check at a time. John's familiar handwriting was scrawled on each check. Many creditors were paid monthly, so she saw Long Island Power Authority, Cablevision, and Long Island Water repeatedly. Lena continued to sift through the boxes of old checks until she saw one written to MHN, Inc. It was for eight hundred dollars.

"What? What's this?" she said as she stared at the odd check, whose payee she didn't recognize.

Lena's chest tightened, and her heartbeat quickened. She felt betrayed, yet she didn't know how or why. Lena had always hated secrets. "They destroy people," she said, "the ones who keep them and the subjects of the secret. No good comes from keeping secrets."

She had to find out more about this MHN, Inc. Lena grabbed her old phone book in the kitchen and sat down to turn to the *M*'s. In no time, she'd found it, scribbled the address on a notepad, grabbed her coat, and shot out the front door on a mission. She'd sat quietly for too long. It was time to find out what was going on.

Half an hour later, Lena walked into Medical Home Nursing, in Suite 402 of a huge medical plaza. Lena had no clue what she'd do or say as she approached the perky receptionist.

"Can I help you?" asked the receptionist.

"Oh, I hope so," Lena began, just as eager to see where her words would go as the receptionist was. "I'm afraid my husband's check will bounce, so I thought I'd come in and pay cash."

"Sure." The girl smiled as she turned to face her computer screen to her right. "Patient name?"

"Um, well, I can't quite—it's just that—uh, my husband's name is John Mastantuono, if that helps."

"Oh! Right! Mama DeFabrizio. Sure, here she is," the girl said as she looked at the payment record on her screen. "Nope, you're fine. This month's payment already posted. Looks like your husband hasn't missed a payment in twenty years."

"That's my husband." Lena smirked. "Takes care of

everybody like it's his job. The man is nothin' if not dependable—and predictable. Thanks for your help."

Lena knew exactly where she'd go next. Fueled by mounting fury, she arrived at Mama D's home in no time, marched up to the door, and rang the bell. Lena heard shuffling footsteps grow louder until the door swung open. After a short exchange, an older, matronly home healthcare nurse let Lena inside.

"Follow me, please," she told Lena.

Sounds of a game show grew louder, and they walked toward the back room. Lena walked over to the loud TV and lowered the volume.

"Mama D, you've got a visitor," the nurse said as she turned toward the elderly woman on the end of a sofa.

Although in her midnineties, Mama D had long, gray hair that was loosely braided. Her milky, dark eyes still showed years of sadness that would never heal, not in this lifetime, anyway.

Lena stood in front of the frail woman, whose face bore evidence of too much pain to revisit. Mama D stared expressionless at Lena, who wasn't sure the woman would understand why she'd come, given her advanced age.

"Mama DeFabrizio, you know who I am, right?" she began.

"So. He finally told you," Mama D interrupted, but without so much as shifting her gaze or changing her facial expression.

"Uh, no. He didn't tell me. I found out," Lena clarified.

"How about some tea, ladies?" the home health aide asked, to end the awkward silence between the women.

At first no one answered. Finally, Lena said, "Yeah. Tea. Good. Let me give you a hand."

Lena followed the dowdy but kindly woman, Betty, into the kitchen. Betty busied herself making tea, while Lena looked at the photo collage on the refrigerator. She instantly gasped and covered her mouth with both hands. Staring back at Lena were old black-and-white photos of Rose, wearing her wedding dress, and a uniformed Johnny on their wedding day. The genuinely happy smile on John's face was like a dagger to Lena's heart. She reached out and touched his lips as tears filled her eyes. Then she saw color snapshots mixed in with the older black-and-whites. One was of Lena carrying a birthday cake with lit candles. Another was of Frank standing beside his new truck. There was John's nephew's graduation, the birth of John's niece, and some Christmas photos from when Frank had been a boy.

Lena gasped and tried to catch her breath. She slowly shook her head in disbelief as she stared at the photos that chronicled her family's life. She felt like she'd been sucker-punched as she struggled to steady herself.

"Yeah. I know," the home health aide agreed. "That's about how I'd be feeling, too."

"I'll pass on the tea, thank you," Lena finally managed.

She felt dazed, as if she were walking through a gray, cloudy maze. Lena walked straight to the front door and through it, and she kept going—right back to her neighborhood and the street she'd known for decades. But Lena sped past her house and slammed on the brakes in front of Gina's home.

Gina was raking leaves from her flower beds into a big pile. Startled, she looked up into the sun as a shadow fell across her. "What the—"

"I trusted you! Like a sister, I trusted you!" Lena shouted.

"Wait, no!" Gina stood up. "Lena, I had no idea about the basement. I didn't know!"

"Yeah? And whattabout Rose's motha? The money? All these years, all of it!" Lena screamed, as decades of pains escaped from within.

"Oh, Jesus." Gina covered her mouth with a gloved hand and stared at Lena.

Lena wagged her index finger in Gina's face as she shouted, "All those years ago! You swore he'd get over it! 'Just a matta of time,' you said!"

"Lena, listen. I believed it then, and I still believe it now!"

"Then you're even dumber than *me*!" Lena screamed as tears ran down her cheeks.

"Oh, Lena. C'mere." Gina wrapped her arms around her and held Lena with gloved hands. "Listen, he lied to me, too.

I promise. He lied to me, too."

As Lena sobbed, the hugging women dropped to their knees together and then onto the leaf pile as Lena's shoulders heaved with her guttural sobs. Decades of hurt flooded out of her, as if a dam had broken. Gina tried to soothe Lena's pain and defuse her hurt and anger. But Lena had erupted like a long-dormant volcano. As she held her sister-in-law, Gina knew there would be casualties.

Later that night, Lena walked into Frank's house. Her face was swollen, and her eyes were red. She walked right past Frank.

"Ma? What's wrong?" he asked, almost afraid to hear an answer.

"You wanna know? How much time do ya have?" she scoffed as she headed to her bedroom and shut the door behind her.

CHAPTER 11

Johnny held the photo with wrinkled, trembling hands as he sat on the workshop's floor, leaning against a wall. Rose wore the same dress in the photo that she'd worn that night in 1944. Although the photo was black-and-white, Johnny remembered the dress was light-blue floral on top and solid navy on the bottom with a thin black belt.

When Rose had worn the dress that evening on the beach, Johnny wrapped his arm around her and pulled her close as the ocean breezes blew through her hair. Johnny loved the scent of the salty air mixed with Rose's subtle floral perfume. He knew he'd miss the scent when he left for the army.

**

Johnny liked to make Rose smile and laugh, so he pretended to hold a microphone as he talked into his fist. "Here he comes in the final stretch! But she's bringing up his flank, and they're both streaking toward the finish line nose to nose, and the winner is—"

He held the imaginary mic toward Rose so she could call the winner, but she sighed and said, "Oh, Johnny, I don't want to watch the submarine races tonight."

"What? Why not? It's free," he joked.

"I'm scared, Johnny, really scared."

"Aw, c'mon now. There's nothin' to be scared of."

"We both know that's not the truth," Rose nervously said, as her eyes begged Johnny not to go.

Johnny tenderly stroked her face under the moonlight as Rose steadied her nerves. She took a deep breath, pulled out the pink medicine bottle from her handbag, and took a tiny sip to quell the butterflies in her stomach.

"Rose, listen. I can't *not* fight for my country. That's not how I'm made. You know that," Johnny said.

Rose forced a smile as Johnny cradled her face in his hands, but then she looked away.

"Hey, look at me," he said. "I'm comin' back. There's nothin' on this earth that can keep me from marryin' you, Rose. Nothin'. We'll be together again soon, I promise."

With tears in her eyes, Rose leaned in to kiss her handsome soldier. Johnny kissed her back hungrily and passionately. There was nothing that would stop him from being with Rose.

*

Johnny inhaled deeply and then released his breath into the silent basement. It may have been quiet, tucked away in the bowels of his house, but Johnny was hardly alone. Ghosts of the past lay all around him as he sat amid Rose's old letters, photos, and the newspaper clippings that had forever immortalized her as a young, raven-haired bride.

His watch told Johnny it was time to go. So, he scooped up all he had left of Rose, replaced it in his footlocker, and threw the old tarp over it. Johnny then kissed two fingers and briefly touched them to the footlocker before turning out the light and shutting the door that would seal Rose inside the workshop until his next visit.

Johnny's aged hands gripped his truck's steering wheel as he drove toward the beach. He knew Kevin would be there. After he parked, Johnny walked toward the bench where Kevin sat on one end, his back to the parking lot. Without a word, Johnny sat on the opposite end of the bench from Kevin, who immediately slapped a manila envelope down on the bench between them.

"There's nothin' there," Kevin said as he stared straight ahead.

Johnny picked up the manila envelope and looked inside. "So, why'd you take it, then?"

"To be sure."

Both men sat and stared at the ocean, lost in their own memories. Finally, Kevin said, "I was sorry to hear Vinny died."

"Oh, c'mon! You hated his guts." Johnny smirked.

"Well, how's Gina doing?"

Without answering Kevin, Johnny got up and walked away. Kevin waited a few minutes as he watched the ocean water lap at the shoreline. Then he stood up, shoved his hands into his pockets, and walked off, too. Before he got to the parking lot, Kevin stopped and turned around to look at the ocean one more time. He stared at the empty boardwalk and remembered when he'd been there with Vinny in 1944.

**

Uniformed soldiers and sailors had been everywhere along the boardwalk that day. Some held girls' the hands. Others had their arms wrapped around their girlfriends' waists.

"Hey, Kevin," Vinny had said when he'd caught up to him. "I hear your old man got you a job on the force. Guess I'd better keep my nose clean, huh?"

"Then you wouldn't be *you*," Kevin sneered.

"Look, I know we got our differences," Vinny said, "but for Johnny's sake, I say we patch 'em up. What d'ya say?"

"For *Johnny's* sake?" Kevin scrunched up his face.

"Yeah. 'I'm talkin' about Rose. She's all alone, you know?" Vinny added.

"Well, her sewin' factory's on my beat. I could swing by and check on her," Kevin said.

"I was thinkin' more like we should take her out. Get her

mind off—"

"Who's *we*?" Kevin interrupted.

"You, me, and Gina," Vinny clarified. "Maybe we can go bowling or catch a movie."

"And that's okay with Gina? She's good with that?" Kevin looked skeptical as he considered Vinny's idea.

"Gina? Sure. She'd die for Johnny. So, she can suffer through a little time with you." Vinny laughed. "Just kiddin', man."

"Eh, I dunno."

"C'mon, Kevin. We all gotta do our part and keep the home fires burnin', right?"

Kevin eyed Vinny, trying to figure out the angle or ulterior motive behind Vinny's offer. But Vinny's expression looked sincere, maybe for the first time.

"Yeah. Sure, why not?" Kevin agreed.

"Atta boy!" Vinny said as he slugged Kevin in the arm to emphasize that he'd made the right decision.

*

Kevin shook off the old memory and realized he'd been rubbing his arm, remembering Vinny's punch that day. He walked over to his car and got behind the wheel as he silently chastised himself for being so naive back on that day.

As Kevin drove home, Johnny headed back to his house with the manila envelope on the seat beside him. He parked and then carried the envelope into his house. As he stepped through the back door, Gina was waiting for him.

"You're a sonofabitch! You know that, big brotha?" she yelled.

"Now what is it, Gina?"

"She found out, Johnny! Lena found out everything you've been doin' behind her back all these years! Mama D. The nurses. All of it. What the hell were you thinkin, Johnny?"

"That's none of your damned business! Not Mama, not her healthcare, and not my marriage!" Johnny shouted as he vigorously shook the envelope at his sister. "And sure as hell not Rose! You hear me?"

"What? What about Rose?" Gina asked. "What's that you're holdin'?"

Johnny inhaled deeply and then pulled out a stack of typed pages from the manila envelope. Gina eyed him curiously but tentatively, unsure of what might come next. Johnny held the paper far enough away so his eyes could focus on the old typewritten page in his hand.

"The deceased was to be married on that day," he read aloud.

"What is that? Lemme see it." Gina snatched the paper from Johnny's hand.

"Coroner's report," Johnny said.

Gina suddenly felt queasy.

"Where'd you get it?" she asked.

"Where d'ya think? Who's always stuck his nose where it

didn't belong? He's about six-foot-two, Irish," he spat as he grabbed the page back from his sister.

"Oh, for God's sake, Johnny! Leave it alone! What do ya think you'll find? You were there. You saw it all, same as everyone. You saw what they did to her house that day!"

Johnny could never forget that awful day in '46 at Mama and Papa D's house. Nassau County police crawled all over that house, like ants at a picnic. They jerked out drawers and emptied them onto the floor and turned them over to look on the bottoms. Closets were ransacked and laundry baskets inspected. Police detectives took samples of the foods in Mama D's refrigerator while another gloved man took samples of all the liquor under Vito's bar. They opened shampoo bottles and smelled the contents of peroxide and rubbing alcohol bottles. Johnny's letters to Rose were all tossed into a box, and the box was sealed and then labeled. Flashbulbs popped everywhere as photos were taken of all the rooms in the DeFabrizio house. At the same time, neighbors gathered outside, speaking in hushed voices as they watched items loaded into unmarked, dark cars and the trunks of police cruisers.

While strangers went through their house and tore apart Rose's bedroom, the DeFabrizio family was interviewed one by one at Mama D's kitchen table. Sobs and wails alternately filled the kitchen, mostly Mama D's. Rookie officer Kevin McCarthy watched from a doorway, and his heart nearly broke in two as he watched Gina's heaving sobs on the sofa. Kevin felt powerless to help Gina as Vinny went and sat beside her. Her face was ashen, and Vinny's was swollen from crying.

Without a word, an officer handed Gina a box of Kleenex tissues. She grabbed one, dabbed her eyes and her nose, and looked at Vinny in desperation. Kevin saw the defeated look in Vinny's eyes as he succumbed to his fate and wrapped an arm around Gina's heaving shoulders. Kevin knew Vinny had resigned himself to being with Gina, as any hopes of being with Rose were forever dashed.

Johnny sat in silent shock in a chair across the living room. He stared at Vinny and watched as his sister clung to the man who'd never treated her as well as Johnny would have liked. Kevin watched all of them until he could take no more, and then he walked outside for some air and watched detectives load brown paper evidence bags into a car's trunk.

Kevin hated that day, all of it. He'd played it over and over in his mind. Mama D's wails had sounded like the cries of a wounded animal, and Gina's guttural sobs had sent her into the bathroom twice to vomit. Pain and sadness hung over the DeFabrizio house, threatening to smother everyone in it.

Kevin forced himself to stop thinking about it, as he'd done for years. Instead, he turned into his driveway and wondered what Johnny thought he could do with the reports in that manila envelope.

*

When Gina finally went home, Johnny sank into an upholstered chair in his too-quiet living room. The small reading lamp beside him was the only light inside his house as Rose's autopsy report lay in his lap. Johnny stared at the paper for hours as time stood still.

The words made him think of young Rose: *The hair is brown, wavy, and ample. The skin is clear.* Johnny shut his eyes and remembered how her hair smelled and how it had felt to run his fingers through it, how he'd lift it to kiss Rose's soft neck.

Johnny had grown tired over the years. Grief had fatigued his brain, and sorrow had weakened his heart. He'd exhausted himself replaying his memories with Rose, in order to not lose them. They were all he had left—except the ghosts in the basement, of course.

**

Johnny thought back to that night in the dunes at the beach. His hands had been in her soft hair as he and Rose kissed. It was one of their most passionate kisses, as they'd hungrily and desperately melded into each other.

"Wait!" Rose pulled away. "What if you don't come back, Johnny?"

"How many times do I have to tell you, I'm comin' back to you," he reassured her.

"But how can we ever know that?" Rose asked as she unbuttoned his shirt and then kissed him passionately again.

Johnny held her close against his bare chest and kissed her. Again, she pulled away, worried about their future.

"What if we never get married, though?" she said. "What if it never happens, and we never get that little Cape Cod with a climbing tree for our kids? What if you never get to plant tomatoes in our garden, or have Sunday dinners with our children?"

"I'll be back," Johnny promised, kissing her again while she slipped off her cardigan and undid the belt on her dress.

"I know you say that, but what if," Rose agonized.

"Don't even think it. We'll be together forever. I promise," Johnny said.

"Oh, Johnny. Hold me. I want you to remember how I feel right now, this minute." Rose took his palm and placed it on her heart. "For you, Johnny. It beats only for you. Never forget it, not ever."

Johnny gently laid her back on the big blanket he'd brought along to the dunes. As the waves lazily kissed the shoreline, Johnny passionately kissed the only girl he'd ever loved. When they made love that night, they both knew they would always remember this one moment together. Seagulls chattered above them as gentle winds blew through the seagrass on the dunes. Johnny and Rose could have stayed there together, hidden away from the world and in each other's arms forever.

*

Memories of that night with Rose lulled Johnny to sleep. If he couldn't touch her skin anymore, he had to hold her in his heart and keep her in his mind's eye. It was all he had left. Johnny dozed in his living room for a couple of hours. He woke up after 2:30 a.m., closed the autopsy report in his lap, and switched off the reading lamp. Johnny then climbed the stairs, got under the cold sheets in his empty bed, and went to sleep again. Morning would come soon enough, and he would have to face his heartbreak all over again, just as he'd done for decades.

CHAPTER 12

Next door to Johnny's house, Lena made coffee in Frank's kitchen. She still wore the pink sleep cap that protected her hairdo and a green pinstriped housecoat that zipped up the front. There were even two silver metal hairclips that held a curl on either side of her face, just as Frank had seen as a kid. But Ma's face had aged, even if her beauty routine hadn't changed. Frank knew her marriage had worn on her over the years as she'd tried to make it work.

Ma had sacrificed so much. She'd looked the other way and had swallowed her pride too many times to count. Ma had even sacrificed on her wedding day. She'd decided not to wear a traditional white wedding dress on the day she married Johnny. Ma knew that the image of a bride, any bride, made

Johnny remember Rose. She wanted Johnny to think only of *her* on their wedding day, without memories of Rose interfering in the nuptials. So, Lena had worn a beautiful two-piece skirt suit to help Johnny get a fresh start toward their future together.

"Busy day, Frank?" Ma asked as she measured ground coffee.

"Oh, yeah," he mumbled as he held a slice of toast in his teeth while pulling on his jacket.

"Okay, I'll throw in some laundry for ya," Ma said.

"Thanks. See ya later, Ma." The front door slammed, and then Frank's house was still and quiet again.

He rushed outside, and as he jumped into his pickup, a figure in his passenger seat startled him. "What the—" Frank exclaimed.

Johnny sat there in dazed silence. He handed the manila envelope to his son and continued to stare out the windshield.

"That's it?" Frank said as he looked in the envelope. Johnny opened the passenger door.

"It's all Greek to me," he said as he got out, shut the door, and walked home without even saying hello to Lena.

Frank couldn't read the reports. He had no time. He needed to contract a new customer and then get his guys started on another job. When he did finally have a few minutes to read the papers inside the envelope, some of the information made no sense. Other notes seemed ambiguous and vague. Frank knew he needed someone to help him make some sense of it all. He made a phone call and then went and dropped the reports off at the hospital, as he was instructed.

Later that afternoon, Frank returned to the Nassau County Medical Center. It was an unsightly, stark brick building that completely lacked character. Trimmed shrubs lined the building's perimeter on the manicured grounds. Doctors and nurses stood clustered near the automatic doors, smoking and chatting during their break time as Frank walked past.

"I'm looking for the Pathology Department," Frank told the volunteer at the information desk.

The elderly man pointed Frank toward a nearby set of elevators and told him to go to the third floor and follow the signs. Frank followed the kindly old man's instructions, and he got on the elevator. As the slow-moving car moved, Frank hoped the head of the Pathology Department had found out something.

Frank stepped out of the elevator and walked the halls until he found Doctor Leitner's office. The door was ajar, but Frank knocked before entering.

"Come in," the doctor said from behind his desk where he'd been reading the coroner's report of Rose's death.

"So?" Frank asked as he took a seat in front of the white-coated, bespectacled doctor.

"Final diagnosis reads: asphyxia due to status asthmaticus," the doctor said.

"In English, please. What's that mean, Doc?" Frank leaned forward in anticipation of getting some answers.

"It basically means they attributed the cause of her death to an asthma attack, but it doesn't make sense to me. There's got to be more to this report than what's here. It's inconclusive in my opinion." The doctor closed the report and slid it across his desk to Frank.

"What do you mean? That's it?" Frank asked in desperation.

The doctor shrugged. "This looks incomplete to me. What do you want me to tell you?"

"Doc, please!" Frank pleaded. "There's gotta be more. You don't know how important this is. You've gotta help me. I'll pay you! Please, just tell me what you need."

The doctor saw the distress in Frank's eyes.

"History," the doctor said. "I'll need more history on the matter. Family history, medical records, anything that can provide some more background on the deceased," he clarified.

Frank told the doctor he'd work on getting more information. But as he walked back to his truck, he had no clue how to possibly do that. As he drove back to a job site to check on his guys' progress, Frank had an idea. He decided to sleep on it until the next day.

*

When Frank walked in to see her, he had no idea what might come of his visit. Mama D beamed as she looked at him, this son of Johnny's who had always held her heart, whether he'd known it or not. Her piercing, dark eyes looked pleased, but Frank couldn't help but notice the framed photo behind the elderly woman. It was a young boy in a Little League uniform with a bat on his shoulder.

"That's me," Frank said, "when I was ten."

Mama D smiled and nodded.

"When'a you a'born, I told'a you papa he gave'a me a grandson," she explained.

But Frank was confused, conflicted, and confounded all at once. Mama D realized he didn't understand, and she continued.

"You see," she said with a glint in her eyes, "in'a my heart, Johnny is'a my son and'a always will'a be."

"Missus DeFab," Frank began.

But Mama touched his hand and said, "You call'a me Mama."

"Mama," he began again. "I need to ask you about Rose."

"Ah, my'a Rosa," she smiled as she clenched her frail hands to her chest.

The two talked for a while, and then Frank excused himself. He needed to go and process their conversation. He also needed to call Doctor Leitner. Frank jumped in his truck and instinctively reached for his cell phone, only to remember he'd smashed it to pieces when he thrown it from a roof into the bed of his pickup.

"Great." He sighed. "Everyone else is stuck back in the 1940s, so why shouldn't I be, too?"

Cars passed his truck as Frank drove along distractedly, lost in his thoughts. Then, in a daze, he rolled through a stop sign without ever seeing it. Tires screeched, horns blew, and the driver of a septic truck gave him the finger. Frank slammed on his brakes and came to rest on the opposite side of the intersection.

"Now, wouldn't that've been perfect if I'd been hit by a septic truck? Why not? Shit's been rainin' down on me for weeks!" he thought.

Frank took a deep breath and adjusted his truck's seat. He then signaled and pulled back onto the road. Up ahead was an old payphone hanging beside the entrance to a bar. Frank parallel parked alongside the curb, dug out some quarters from his console, and pulled a business card from his pocket. He jumped out and made his call.

"Doctor Leitner, please. It's Frank Mastantuono."

"This is Doctor Leit—" he soon heard.

"Doc, you got a pen?" Frank eagerly interrupted. "Take this down."

*

Meanwhile, Johnny was home alone. Well, not exactly *alone*

since the ghosts of Rose never left him. As he rolled an old cue ball in his right palm, Johnny thought back to when he had come home from the war. He could almost hear Glen Miller playing on the jukebox as pool balls clacked and popped on the nearby pool table.

Johnny and Rose had walked into Willow Tavern that night holding hands. He'd worn his uniform, and all eyes were on him.

**

"Johnny! Hey! Look who's back! someone yelled. Suddenly hands came from all directions as everyone congratulated Johnny, shook his hand, and welcomed him home from the war.

Someone slapped him on the back with gusto. "Welcome home, soldier!" a voice said as someone squeezed Johnny's shoulder.

Rose beamed as she stepped out of the way to allow everyone time with Johnny. But she could tell her fiancé didn't like all the attention. Johnny never cared for the spotlight, not when he'd won a football game for his team or when his mother made a big deal of his good grades. So, he felt awkward coming home from war and being the center of attention. Humble and pragmatic, Johnny had always thought he wasn't anything special, just a guy who preferred to make good choices and live honorably.

"Hey, soldier! Buy you a drink?" the gruff, grizzled

bartender called out as he polished a glass.

Relieved to have an escape route, Johnny nodded at the bartender and made his way through the sea of people. "You're a sight for sore eyes, Jack," Johnny said as he shook Old Jack's hand.

"Then they must be pretty sore," Jack laughed. "What can I getcha, Johnny? On the house, whateva you want."

"Bourbon. Straight," he said.

Rose walked up to the empty barstool beside Johnny and sat down. "Hey, you never used to drink bourbon," she said.

"Lotta things I never used to do." And with that, Johnny tipped back the shot glass, and tossed back the best bourbon Jack stocked.

"Hey, look." Rose nodded toward a group of people that had just come in. "There's Vinny and Gina. C'mon."

"You go," Johnny said. "Grab us a booth, and I'll be right over."

"You sure?" Rose hesitated as she slid from her barstool.

"Yeah. Go on. I'll get us some drinks."

Rose smiled and went to talk to Gina and Vinny. Johnny leaned on the bar with his weight on his forearms. Suddenly, loud laughter from a raucous group startled Johnny, and he nearly jumped out of his skin.

"You all right there, soldier?"

"Yeah, sure," Johnny said, straightening up when he noticed the man's uniform. "I mean, sir, yes, *sir!*"

"At ease, private," the officer said. "Why aren't you with your friends?"

Johnny looked down and shrugged. "Just takin' a minute to myself, sir."

"Well, it takes longer than that, son."

"What does?" Johnny asked.

"They'll never understand. They can't. It's like they live in a different world where they have no idea about what nearly happened to them. If not for the gunpowder and fortitude—"

"And *blood*," Johnny said glumly.

The army captain nodded in agreement as Johnny watched all the happy, laughing, and relaxed people inside the tavern. He saw that Rose had settled into a booth with Vinny and Gina.

"Give it some time, it'll get better. In the meantime, just rest easy in the fact that you helped save the world. For that, we all thank you, soldier." The captain held up two fingers, and Jack came over with the good bottle of bourbon and refilled their glasses. The two men raised their glasses to each other, clinked them together, and swiftly knocked back their drinks.

A few rounds later, Johnny slurred out, "Thank you, sir." He then saluted the captain and staggered over to say hello to his sister and Vinny, seated with Rose in a booth. But he felt out of place, and like he didn't belong there with everyone else. Something had changed within him, and Johnny felt like an outsider. He excused himself to go to the men's room, but on the way, Johnny spied the piano off to the side of the bar.

He went over and sat on the bench, the one he had sat on years before, and began playing the first tune that came into his head. At first, patrons watched and listened appreciatively to the musical stylings of the handsome soldier. A couple of uniformed flyboys walked over and stood on either side of Johnny as his calloused fingers clumsily manipulated the piano keys—not quite like his music teacher at church had taught him as a boy.

Rose watched miserably from across the tavern as she sat with Vinny and Gina. Johnny was drunk like she'd never seen him before. Rose knew he wasn't the same since he returned, but he wouldn't talk to her. She'd heard that some soldiers had issues reintegrating into society, but if Johnny wouldn't tell her what was bothering him, she couldn't help him.

Frustration blanketed Rose as she listened to Johnny and the flyboys belt out the lyrics to "We'll Meet Again" while Johnny led them on the piano. "*Smiling through, just like you always do . . .* ," they drunkenly crooned, as other patrons joined in with the anthem of hope.

"He's just blowin' off a little steam's all," Gina told Rose.

"More like blowin' *us* off, I'd say," Vinny corrected. "Who wants to hit the road?"

"We will do no such thing," Rose instructed. She then

jumped up and went over to Johnny just as he finished the song.

"Johnny? It's getting late."

But he didn't answer Rose. Instead, Johnny slung an arm over her shoulder and drunkenly hung on her as he tried to focus his eyesight. Rose leaned into him to try and steady him.

"Hey, guys!" Johnny slurred. "This is my girl! Best girl in the world. Wrote to me every day!"

"Sure sign of a guilty conscience," one flyboy snickered to the other.

"I'll say," the other agreed, and then they clanked their glasses and then broke into laughter.

"Oh, no, no, no, no," Johnny slurred as he spoke in the direction of the flyboys. He couldn't focus on their faces but knew they were there. "*No*, not my Rose. She's not sittin' under the apple tree with anyone but *me*. Not that my buddies didn't try, mind you. Bunch'a damned dogs. Don't even know you gotta respect a girl if you wanna love her. That's what Mama said."

"C'mon. Let's get you out of here. You've had enough, Johnny."

"You mean that *you've* had enough—*of me*," Johnny slowly slurred as he crossed his feet and nearly tripped. "Of *me*," he added again, followed by a bourbon belch that made Rose lean away from him even as she held onto Johnny. She tried to steer him toward the door, but not with much luck.

"Okay, enough," Rose said as she unwrapped herself from under Johnny's arm and stomped to her booth. Without a word, Rose snatched up her cardigan and her purse, and she stormed toward the door.

Vinny made a move to follow her, but Gina grabbed his arm. "Let her go!" she said. Vinny took his seat again and they watched Rose make her way through the crowd.

"Hey. What's wrong?" Kevin asked when Rose bumped into him. He was in his police blues.

"Johnny. He's acting crazy."

"They all act crazy when they come home. He'll come out of it. Just give it time. Wait a while," Kevin said.

"Wait? I've *waited* nearly two years for tonight, for this very night when he'd come home to me."

Kevin looked down at her and winked. "Listen, I'll get him home for you."

Rose watched as Kevin walked through the crowd and made his way toward the piano. Johnny stopped playing and looked up at Kevin. He leaned back and squinted, as he tried to get a better look at Kevin's face.

"Johnny! Welcome home, man!" Kevin said.

Johnny made a face and sarcastically said, "Yeah. *You* really missed me, didn't you?"

"Sure." Kevin shrugged. "We all did." Kevin was confused by Johnny's remark.

The flyboys eyed him with cautious contempt. Kevin knew they thought he was messing with their new army buddy and might have to step in since Johnny was in no state to handle anything.

"Nice uniform, Kevin," Johnny slurred. "Don't s'pose you got any blood on it."

The flyboys busted out in laughter as Johnny turned his attention back to the piano and began playing "Beer Barrel Polka." Johnny's nimble fingers flew across the keys and jumped with the exaggerated enthusiasm of a showman.

"Come on, Johnny," Kevin urged. "I promised Rose that I'd get you home."

"You hear that, guys?" Johnny yelled to the Flyboys. "*He* promised *my* girl!"

The guys at the bar laughed and raised their glasses to Johnny and he switched to his favorite song, "More Than You Know." Couples instantly took the floor while people all around joined in to sing the popular song. But Kevin got the message. He walked away, a mix of humiliation and confusion, and went to find Rose.

"Sorry, Rose. I tried. Come on. I'll take you home." He helped her on with her sweater, motioned for Rose to walk in front of him, and then followed her out the door.

Vinny grinned as he watched them leave together. He excitedly grabbed Gina's hand, and he jitterbugged the two of them onto the floor to join the other dancing couples.

"What's gotten into you?" Gina laughed.

"Just havin' a great night is all!" Vinny grinned.

But Gina leaned back and looked at him, uncertain of why the stick-in-the-mud had suddenly become the life of the party.

CHAPTER 13

Hours later, Gina steered a drunken Johnny to the front porch of their parents' house—but not before he had stripped off his army uniform and slung it on the lawn. Gina had tried to stop him as she stooped to pick up his clothes while nervously watching for their neighbors.

"Enough, Johnny! Cut it out right now!" Gina said.

All at once, her brother stopped staggering, dropped to all fours, and threw up with a force that made Gina jump out of the way. Since Johnny was otherwise occupied, Gina pulled out a cigarette, lit it, and took a deep drag. Johnny called for Jesus to help him as his body wracked and heaved. But Gina couldn't sympathize with her big brother. She eyed him coldly and shook her head with one hand on her hip and a cigarette in the other.

"You're a real asshole," Gina said, showing Johnny no mercy. "How could you treat her like that? What's wrong with you?"

But Johnny couldn't speak. He alternately puked and then tried to catch his breath before he vomited some more. Gina was relentless, though, and she wouldn't let up. Her brother was her captive audience, and she'd make sure he heard what she had to say.

"I wouldn't blame her if she never talked to you again, Johnny."

Those words hit hard. Johnny glanced up at Gina with a look of sober realization that told her he'd finally heard her and knew what he had done.

"Is that what you want, Johnny?" she continued. "Do you really want Rose to leave you? Because that's exactly what'll happen if you ever pull this shit again!"

Johnny wanted to ask her to stop yelling at him, but when he opened his mouth, he passed out with his head resting on the bottom step of their porch. Gina shook her head as she picked up Johnny's jacket and covered her brother.

"Sleep tight," she whispered as she noticed a letter that had fallen out of Johnny's pocket.

Gina unfolded the wrinkled letter and began to read it. It started with generalities and niceties and was peppered with some local gossip. Gina found it odd that Vinny had taken the time to write to Johnny while he had been away. She kept reading until she got to the last paragraph.

*

And don't you worry about Rose. Kevin is always around and he's taking <u>real good</u> care of her. (Maybe too good if you ask <u>me</u>.) I just hope you get home soon, buddy, if you know what I mean.

*

Gina had no idea when she slipped Vinny's letter into her pocket back then that she would ever pick it up again. But as she stared at her wedding portrait one afternoon, fifty-five years later, the indifferent, unaffected look in Vinny's eyes made her blood boil. She lit a cigarette and then held her lighter beneath the letter until the center of the paper caught fire. Gina watched the flame grow taller as the paper browned and ashes dropped. She laid the letter in a nearby ashtray and stared at it until there was nothing left.

"If only it had been that easy," she thought.

Startled from her daze, Gina heard the familiar sound of her nephew Paul's Camaro outside. But the sound got quieter, so Gina realized he'd gone on to his parents' house. She wondered if Paul knew his parents had been arguing and that Debbie had moved out.

Nineteen-year-old Paul jumped out of his car in Frank's driveway and grabbed a gigantic laundry bag from his backseat. Sporting a faux hawk with lots of hair on top and shaved sides, Paul wore a single herringbone gold chain around his neck and brand-new, super-clean Nike sneakers.

He walked right into the house without knocking or ringing the bell.

"It's my favorite girl!" Paul grinned when he saw Lena in Frank's kitchen.

"Paul?"

"No, Grandma, it's Old Blue Eyes," he laughed as he hugged her and lifted her off the ground to dance with her. Lena laughed and smiled as he twirled her around his parents' kitchen.

"Put me down! I got sausage and peppers goin' over there!" she protested.

"So, you're livin' here now, Grandma?" Paul asked as he eyed her sideways.

"Not somethin' I care to discuss."

Paul saw a row of aluminum pans lining the kitchen counter. "What's all this?" he asked.

"I'm volunteering down at the American Legion hall," Lena said. "Somethin' I've always wanted to do."

"How 'bout if you volunteer at St. Johns?" Paul suggested as he grabbed a sausage from a tray with his fingers. "Really, Grandma. I'm starvin' to death at school."

"I'll make you something to eat."

"No, I can't stay, Grandma. I just came by to grab some stuff for Ma."

"What kinda stuff?" Lena asked.

"Clothes. Her jewelry box. Her winter coat. You know,

stuff," Paul said.

Lena nodded and said, "Sounds like a woman who's not comin' back."

Paul nodded in agreement, saying nothing to the contrary.

"Divorce is a sin. You know?" Lena said.

"The way my dad treated us is a sin."

"Really? 'Cause the last time I looked, he bought you a brand-new car and those chains around your neck, and he sent you to that fancy school. I'll bet he even bought you those hideous shoes on your feet, too."

"Yeah, the American Dream, right?" Paul then looked down at his feet. "Hey! Whats'a matta with my new shoes? These are Air Jordans."

Lena didn't answer her grandson. Instead, she bent over and picked up Paul's overstuffed laundry bag and lugged it to the washing machine.

Paul looked around Frank's kitchen and said, "What? No bread for the sausage, Grandma? Whats'a guy gotta do to get a sandwich in this house?"

Lena dropped the laundry bag and went back to the kitchen. She rolled her eyes as she grabbed a fresh hero roll from a basket and began stuffing it with sausage and peppers. Paul grinned at the grandmother, who'd always doted on her family. She was one of the reasons he came back as often as he did.

After he ate, Paul pushed back from the table. "Amazing,

as usual," he proclaimed.

"Well, give me notice next time, and I'll have meatballs for you to take back with you—so you don't starve to death. Now go and get your mother's things," Lena said.

Twenty minutes later, Paul carried his mom's full suitcase, along with her winter coat on its hanger, to his car. But he stopped dead in his tracks and his jaw dropped open.

"Grandpa? What're you doin?" he asked as he looked past Johnny to his sudsy Camaro, while his grandfather stood holding a sponge and a garden hose.

"Whaaat? It's filthy. Look at this. How'd you let it get like this? Haven't I taught you to take care of your stuff like you got some pride? Look over there at my yard, Paul. Rich, green grass, perfectly manicured, mowed, and edged to perfection. I even keep the hedges trimmed, and I check 'em to make sure they're even. It matters, believe me!"

Before Paul could speak, Johnny added, "So, what happened to this car? How'd you get it like this?"

"Practice," he shrugged. "So, you're in the doghouse, huh, Grandpa?"

Johnny dismissively waved his weathered hand at Frank's house and asked, "What'd you eat in there?"

"Sausage and peppers. Some of her best yet."

Johnny sighed longingly. "Yeah? I'm livin' on canned tuna and tomato soup ova there."

"Sounds like college." Paul laughed. "Got any girls over

there?"

"You don't wanna know." As he sprayed water on the Camaro to rinse it, Johnny nodded at the suitcase and said, "Looks like the Mastantuono women are startin' to wake up, eh?"

*

As Paul drove his mom's belongings to her, Frank picked up a job. Brooding and lost in thought, he coiled ropes while Bobby, his helper, walked the gable roof collecting loose nails. Finally, Bobby spotted something at the edge of a dormer and walked closer to inspect it.

"Hey, why'd you trim the flashing there?" he asked Frank.

"What? Who the fuck trims flashing?"

But Bobby squatted down and then felt under the bottom row of shingles. "It's missing," he told Frank. "Yep, missing."

"No way. Impossible," Frank said.

"Aw, shit. Man, we've gotta rip it all apart." Bobby sighed as he rested his chin on his chest in defeat. "Jesus, Mister M. I know your name's on the truck and all, and that you're hard up with your wife, but—"

"Don't even go there!" Frank yelled.

Bobby shut up, but he was irritated that he'd be working longer because Frank had been distracted. He went to grab more nails as he considered whether he should just quit.

Later that night, Frank dropped Bobby at home and then drove over to Willow Tavern. What was the point in hurrying home? Debbie wasn't there. So instead, Frank thought a beer was in order, especially after the day he'd had. He walked inside, holding the door for a woman who was leaving, and looked around for an empty seat. He spied an empty booth and slid into one side of it.

A cocktail waitress smiled to let Frank know she'd seen him, and moments later, she hurried over to get his order.

"Whatever's on tap is fine," he told her. "And keep 'em comin', please."

Frank was so distressed and tired that he hadn't even noticed the pretty waitress flirting with him. He couldn't remember the last full night's sleep he'd had. All he did was lie in his big, empty bed and stare at the ceiling and try to make sense of all that had happened. Eventually, the sun always rose, and Frank dragged himself from his bed and into a shower.

By the time he'd ordered his fourth beer, Frank felt better about things. After his sixth beer, he was confident that he could work out all the issues for everyone in his family. When he had emptied his seventh beer glass, Frank thought he needed to rest his eyes and think about things for a bit. He slid low in the booth, crossed his arms on his chest, and shut his eyes.

"Tough luck, McCarthy!" a voice mockingly said later.

Frank opened his eyes and listened for a minute as he watched Sharon, the buxom cocktail waitress, as she carried a tray of drinks to a table. But Frank wasn't interested in anything but the man who played pool behind him. He slid out of the booth and willed himself to stand up straight. When he walked over, he saw Kevin McCarthy running the table and making every shot, aware of all the eyes on him. As Kevin lined up his final shot, he glanced toward Frank, who waited and watched in the shadows.

CRACK!

Kevin sent the eight ball hard and fast into a corner pocket. Then he scooped a twenty-dollar bill off the table's rail and walked over to the bar and laid the money down.

"Gimme a beer," he said to the bartender. "And whatever he's having," Kevin added as he pointed his thumb over his head and behind him at Frank.

Frank walked over and sat down beside Kevin on a barstool, leaving two seats open between Kevin and himself. The bartender placed a cold beer in front of Frank, walked a few steps, and put another frosted glass down in front of Kevin. Both men tipped back their glasses in unison and then silently set them down, constantly facing forward.

"So, what do you want?" Kevin finally asked.

"I'm Johnny's son, Frank."

"I know who you are. What do you *want?*"

"Information. About Rose."

"Ah! So, you're the dumb bastard who kicked this off again," Kevin said.

Frank shook his head and sighed. "Don't think I'm happy about it, not at all."

"Then let it drop." Kevin exhaled hard and then gulped his beer.

Frank drank his beer. He said nothing else to Kevin.

"What d'ya want to know?" Kevin finally asked.

*

Johnny knew he wouldn't be able to sleep. He ate his last can of tomato soup for dinner, but he was still hungry. He wondered what Lena had made for dinner next door. After a shower, Johnny grabbed a book and went to bed to read. As he stared at the ceiling, he thought about the time again, right after he'd returned from the army, when he'd foolishly gotten drunk and had upset Rose.

**

He'd enlisted Celia's help to make things right again with Rose. It had been easy to ask Mama and Papa D to give him some time in their house alone with Rose.

"I need to fix this," he told Mama D.

"You'a do whatever its'a gonna take, Johnny. Rosa love'a you and'a you love'a Rosa. Some people'a meant to be together. Thats'a all a'that a'matters!"

"Rose? Rose, wake up," Celia said in her cheerful, singsong voice. "It's getting cold."

Rose tried to open her puffy eyes as she rubbed her salt-stained cheeks. "What? Celia? What're you doing here?"

"I helped Johnny make your surprise breakfast," Celia said proudly.

Rose instantly sat upright in her bed and stared wide-eyed at Johnny's sister as Celia handed her a robe from a nearby chair and then ran out of the bedroom. Suddenly, Rose deeply inhaled, certain she smelled burnt toast—and maybe even burnt bacon. She slipped on her robe and quickly ran a brush through her hair.

"Here, Rose." Celia smiled as she handed her a wet washcloth. "Gina tells me to wash my face if I cry. This will wipe away your sad eyes."

Rose smiled at Celia as she wiped her face with the wet cloth. She'd always adored Celia's kind spirit and eagerness to make others feel better. Rose couldn't imagine Celia any way other than how God had made her. She was a gift to everyone she'd ever met.

"Gina's right!" Rose said after she'd wiped her face. "I feel much better." Celia looked pleased as she took Rose's hand and led her downstairs to the kitchen.

The smells of burnt toast and burnt bacon became stronger, and when Rose rounded the corner to the kitchen, her suspicions were confirmed. Johnny had opened the back door and was feverishly fanning the air with a folded newspaper. Rose laughed as she took a seat at the table. A single red rose sat in a bud vase in front of a china plate of blackened toast, bacon that looked more like dehydrated jerky, and watery eggs that could be eaten through a straw.

"I'm afraid I might've used too much coffee," Johnny said as he placed a cup of dark, thick sludge in front of Rose's plate.

"You can never have enough caffeine in the morning." Rose smiled.

"I guess I've got a lot to learn."

"We both do," she agreed.

Johnny smiled gratefully at the only girl he'd ever loved.

"Johnny, I didn't know who you were. All the drinking, the attitude, the way you shut me out. I've never seen you like that, and I don't want to ever see it again."

"I get it. Really, I do," he said as he dropped to his knee beside her chair. "Rose DeFabrizio, will you marry me?"

"You already asked me." Rose laughed. "And I said yes."

"Please, say it again. Rose, tell me again that you'll marry me."

Rose sighed deeply, made a face, and said, "On one condition."

"Anything! Name it!"

"I do all the cooking," she said, nodding at the mess in the kitchen with dirty pans, bowls, utensils, and spilled coffee grounds everywhere.

"Yes, please." Johnny laughed.

Celia ran back into the kitchen, beaming with happiness that Johnny and Rose were smiling and laughing again. She was proud that she'd had a hand in helping Johnny to fix things with Rose. Celia loved helping everyone, but when Johnny had asked for her help, she'd felt important and special. She figured that was how Johnny made Rose feel, too.

"Anyone for breakfast?" Johnny laughed. "Let's go down to the diner and get some food that's edible."

"Five minutes," Rose said as she got up from the table to go and change.

"And maybe tonight you and I can go down to the shore," Johnny whispered as he kissed Rose's cheek.

"Oh? Are they having the submarine races again?" She laughed as she blushed.

An hour later, the close-knit trio sat in the diner laughing and joking together. They didn't notice Gina outside the plate glass window, carrying a sack of groceries. She was going to get their attention, but instead, she stopped and just watched from outside.

"Thank you," she whispered as she made the sign of the cross and then looked skyward.

CHAPTER 14

When Johnny walked into his house one evening, he found it still, empty, and too quiet. He wondered when Lena would be finished being angry with him. He wasn't sure, but he had plenty of time to ponder the question.

Johnny opened the refrigerator and found a partial stick of butter, a slice of bologna, a head of brown lettuce, and two bottles of beer. He sighed and shut the fridge door, and then checked the pantry for options. Fortunately, he still had some storm rations from the winter they kept on hand in case they lost power.

Johnny grabbed a can of Spaghetti-O's, opened it with a can opener, and ate right from the can. "Less clean-up. No dishes," he rationalized as he grabbed a beer from the refrigerator. Johnny stood in the kitchen leaning against a counter and eating his dinner. He'd never felt more alone in all his life.

Johnny's eyes fell on the basement door, and he forced himself to look away. But the door pulled him back, and he couldn't take his eyes off it. He knew he shouldn't go down there, but he couldn't help it. By the time he'd finished eating his Spaghetti-O's, he decided to allow himself just a quick visit downstairs.

Five minutes later, Johnny was in his basement's workshop. He pulled out the footlocker and opened it to its familiar, well-handled contents. He'd done a lot of thinking lately, both about the future and the past. When he reached down and picked up an old 8x10 black-and-white photo, Johnny wistfully recalled the day it was taken back in '46.

**

Everyone had been so happy at the backyard celebration. Flashbulbs went off all around, and countless photos were taken. But the photo that Johnny now held had been taken from a higher vantage point, as if the photographer had climbed a tall ladder to get a wider overall shot of the partygoers at the DeFabrizio home.

There were jugs of wine in wicker baskets, fresh breads, and beautiful flowers all around. Mama D had cooked for days, and everyone feasted on lasagna, salads, and more desserts than anyone could count. Old men played bocce on the lawn while children chased each other around the tableclothed picnic tables.

Johnny stood on a bench and tapped his wineglass with a knife. "Everybody! If I can just get your attention for a second!" A hush fell over the crowd as everyone turned to face Johnny. "I just want to thank all of you for coming. And I want to thank Mama D for cooking her heart out all week and putting all this together for us!"

"Grazie! Grazie, Mama!" people said as wineglasses clinked around the backyard.

"But most of all, I want to thank Rose. There were a lot of lonely, scary nights when I didn't think I'd make it until dawn. But then I'd think of Rose, and—" Johnny got choked up and had to clear his throat. "And I'd think of Rose, and I'd see her face and her smile, and I knew I'd do anything to get back to her so we could start our life together."

"Awwww," the crowd cooed.

There wasn't a dry eye around him as Johnny raised his glass to salute Rose, the strong young woman with the kind heart who gave Johnny's life meaning. She walked over to him, and he extended his hand to help her step onto the bench beside him. They held hands as Johnny continued speaking.

"Anyhow, Rose and I have an announcement to make. Don't we, Rose?" he smiled as he looked over at her, and she squeezed his hand tighter to give him strength.

"Rose and I have decided," Johnny said slowly, "that right

after our honeymoon"—he paused, hesitant to deliver the punchline—"we will be moving to Yonkers!"

Johnny raised his glass, but the crowd fell silent. Everyone looked crestfallen. They looked around at each other, unsure of what to say or how to feel.

Gina looked like she'd just learned of a death in the family. Celia panicked and reached for her brown medicine bottle to calm her nerves. Vinny swore under his breath. And Mama D looked around at all the stunned faces in her backyard as they tried to imagine life without their favorite couple.

Finally, Mama D shook her head and quietly said, "Buona fortuna," and then she went inside and closed the door.

*

Later that night, Gina and Johnny were at their parents' home. Gina hadn't said much after Johnny's surprise announcement had left everyone speechless. She'd been thinking about what her life would be like if Johnny left Inwood.

"So, what about *me*, Johnny?" she asked as she slammed a kitchen drawer shut. "What am *I* supposed to do?"

"C'mon, Gina. It's Yonkers for God's sake, not Alaska! It's just ninety minutes away. I have a great job opportunity there with an army buddy"

"It might as well be Alaska! You think Vinny will stick around now?"

"If he knows what's good for him," Johnny joked.

"You don't get it! Listen, Johnny. Mama and Papa are gone. They left us the house, and you're the man of the house, the head of our family. You're supposed to stay here —in Inwood!"

Suddenly, the walls closed in around him, and Johnny felt claustrophobic and as if his clothes were too tight. His face felt hot as he tried not to get angry with his sister.

"What? When did I sign on for that?" he asked. "You know I love you guys, but I want to have a life and build a future with my new wife!"

"Yeah? You think I don't want the same, Johnny?" Gina yelled as she stormed out of the kitchen and past Celia.

"Celia," Johnny said as he noticed her shaking hands trying to open her brown medicine bottle. "Hey, are you okay?"

"I'm getting nerves, Johnny," she anxiously said.

"Here, let me." He took the bottle and opened it for her. Celia tipped it back and took a big sip.

"Hey, use a spoon," he reminded her.

"Sorry, Johnny. I forgot," said Celia.

"You do understand why I have to leave, though. Don't you?" Johnny asked.

"No, I don't. What did I do, Johnny?"

"What? No! No, Celia, you didn't do anything. You could never do anything that would make me want to be away from you. It's just things change when people get married. It's like starting a new adventure together. Do you understand?"

Johnny looked at his sister hopefully as his words sunk in.

"No, I don't understand. Can I come to Yonkers, too? I want an adventure, Johnny."

"Well, sure. Yonkers isn't that far. You can come to visit any time you'd like."

"But I don't want to visit. I want to live with you, Johnny."

Johnny ran his hand through his hair, unsure of how to deal with Celia so her feelings wouldn't be hurt. Finally, he said, "Sorry, sweetie, but I'll be starting a new job and will be really busy working. You've gotta stay here and take care of Gina. She needs you."

"But Vinny is a shithead," Celia said.

Johnny burst out laughing, but then he caught himself and stopped.

"Aw, he's all right. You'll see. Plus, this is a big house to take care of, Celia. You're the big sister, remember. We need you here."

She shrugged and said, "If you say so, Johnny."

SLAM!

Gina stormed out the front door. Johnny watched as she stomped down their driveway, obviously furious at someone or something. Celia remained unaffected as she drew a picture in her sketchbook. She knew she could give Gina a wet washcloth later to wipe away her sad eyes to make everything right again.

*

On a warm afternoon, Gina decided to take flowers down to the cemetery. She grabbed a pair of scissors and then walked down to Johnny's house, but his truck wasn't in the driveway. So, she walked around to the backyard to help herself to some flowers from Johnny's gardens. He usually had blooming flowers and ripe vegetables in the bordered gardens near the basement door. But Gina saw the garden had recently been hoed and raked in preparation for new plantings. There were only a few blooming plants, but Gina clipped some pink, yellow, and lavender-colored blooms and took them back to her house.

An hour later, Gina pulled her car through the cemetery gates and drove along the winding road to the massive shade tree that stood protectively over the manicured grounds. She parked, grabbed a shawl she had worn as a young girl from her back seat, and then walked over to the simple marble headstone.

Celia Mary Mastantuono
Beloved sister, adoring aunt, child of God
1922–1983

Gina placed the flowers in the metal urn in front of the headstone as tears filled her eyes. She stood staring at her elder sister's name and remembering Celia's sweet, pure heart and the smile that lit up a room like no other.

"Child of God," Gina said. "That you were, Celia. A child of God, created in His perfection and sent to save us sinners."

Gina swallowed hard and then bowed her head and shut her eyes to pray. She prayed for Celia and for their parents, and she asked for guidance and direction. "God, tell me what to do. Show me the answers."

"Amen," she said as she made the cross symbol from her head and then across her chest. She draped the shawl, with its handstitched needlework, over the marble headstone, and then Gina turned away and solemnly walked back to her car.

Gina drove toward home in silence, without even turning on the car radio. Thoughts of the last few decades filled her head. She'd done the best she could, given the situation, to protect her family. With Mama and Papa gone, the family was smaller, and she couldn't bear to lose anyone else.

*

Days later, Frank was inside his house one morning when he heard the familiar sound of the mail truck outside. He lumbered across his lawn as the bathrobe he wore hung open, revealing his boxer shorts underneath. Frank still wasn't used to having to slip on a robe in his own house, but Ma had become a permanent fixture, and he didn't have much choice in the matter. He had also gained a couple of pounds, thanks to Ma's constant cooking and baking. Frank decided that a few pounds were okay. Besides, he knew he'd sweat off the extra weight at work.

Frank waved at the postman, whose truck was stopped next door at his parents' mailbox. He pulled the stack of letters and trade magazines from his mailbox, and as Frank walked back inside, he looked at his mail as he thumbed through the envelopes. When he saw one from St. John's University, he immediately tore it open and then made a beeline to his bedroom to put on some clothes.

"Ma! I'll be back!" he called out before he left.

Fifteen minutes later, Frank's truck tore out of his driveway, throwing gravel everywhere as he gassed it. He could have called, but it wouldn't be the same. A personal visit was in order for this one. The more Frank thought about the letter on the seat beside him, the angrier he grew and the heavier his right foot became on the gas pedal. In no time, his truck turned onto the campus.

Frank's jaw clenched tight as he stomped into the dorm building, as a small group of students parted to let him pass. He didn't even notice them. He was on a mission and had tunnel vision as he stomped toward the door at the end of the hallway.

Without knocking, he threw the door open and walked over and yanked the headphones off Paul's head.

"Pop? What the hell?" Paul mouthed. But Frank couldn't hear him, since the headphone's cord had pulled out of the Yamaha keyboard, too, and loud music blared out all at once inside the small dorm room. The sleeping lump in the other bed still did not move. Frank wondered if it was Paul's roommate or a large laundry pile.

Paul looked at his dad in shock and yelled over the pumping music, "What the hell's goin' on, Pop?"

"You, tell me!" Frank yelled as he waved the envelope in front of Paul.

Paul looked confused.

"Academic probation?" Frank hollered. "I know that I'm just a stupid guinea, but I'm pretty sure this means you're flunkin' out!"

The lump suddenly moved. All at once, an arm shot out from under the comforter and grabbed nearby eyeglasses. In two steps, Paul's roommate bolted from the room. Frank was reminded of when he was a kid and his friends' parents started yelling at them. Kids always know when it's their cue to make a hasty exit and save themselves from the deluge of an angry parent.

"Turn off that fuckin' noise!" Frank yelled.

"It's not noise! It's what I do!" Paul hollered as he lowered the volume.

"No, Paul! You flunk outta school, and you're gonna shoot nails into roofs for the rest'a your life! Is that what you want?"

Paul swallowed hard, obviously deciding which way he should go with his defense. "So, I guess I should become a lawyer? Or a banker? Because that's what *you* want me to do?"

"Yes!"

"C'mon, Pop. My music is still construction and creativity. It's different nails and different tools, but I'm still buildin' and makin' improvements in the world!"

Frank scrunched up his face as he desperately tried to find the words.

"You got no idea about the real world, kid. Not a fuckin' clue! Dreams are for children. Adults deal in reality!"

Paul stood up and faced down his dad. "I want to be a musician. I'm gonna be a musician—a *working* musician."

"Not on my dime, you're not!"

"It's what I'm good at!" Paul yelled.

"Then get good at somethin' else!" And with that, Frank spun around and stormed out. He said nothing to Paul's shivering, shirtless roommate in the hallway. Again, students parted to let Frank pass. They'd seen that parental expression before and knew not to challenge it.

Paul was furious. He felt like he could tear apart the whole dorm room and smash everything in his reach. As his roommate climbed back into his bed, Paul replaced his headphones and went back to playing his keyboard to calm himself.

Frank aimed his truck toward home and put the pedal to the metal once again. But when he turned onto his street, he drove past his home. He didn't want to go into his house and unload his newest problem on Ma. So, instead, he pulled into Gina's driveway.

Five minutes later, Gina made some Sanka as she listened to her nephew tell her about his son. She handed Frank the creamer and a mug of steaming coffee as he sat in her kitchen.

"Failin' a few classes isn't the end of the world," Gina said, trying to be the voice of reason. Frank took a drink and thought about it.

"Eh, maybe." He sighed. "I mean, it's not like anybody died or anything."

Gina swallowed hard, took a sip from her mug, and then smacked the kitchen counter with her hand. "Okay, listen. Frank, I love you, but you're like a bull in a china shop. So, maybe, instead of bustin' everything you touch, you could try fixin' what you've already broken."

He shook his head and thought about it. "Thanks for the coffee, Aunt Gina," Frank said as he got up with his mug and headed for the door.

"Hey, bring that back later, okay? You've got lots'a my dishes down there already," Gina called after him as Frank left.

"Yeah. I'll tell Ma to fill 'em before I return them to you. My refrigerator is gonna explode with all the food she's got in there. It's more than I eat in three months—well, since Debbie left, anyway."

Frank shook his head in disgust and climbed in his truck. He couldn't believe his family was falling part around him. Life had gone crazy, and nothing was as he had known it. The Mastantuono women were changing. The world was changing, and Inwood was changing. Frank wished he could return to his prior oblivious state where all seemed well with the world. But those days seemed so long ago.

CHAPTER 15

He needed to talk to Debbie, although she'd shot down his other attempts to have a conversation. But Frank wasn't ready to give up. He sipped coffee from a paper cup as he sat behind the wheel of his truck and eyed the door of the Hair Today salon.

Minutes later, Debbie emerged from the shop, locked the door, and walked to her car. The streetlights had just come on as Frank started his engine. He waited for her car to pull onto the road and then followed behind at a careful distance. Debbie soon turned into a garden apartment complex. Frank stopped and watched her car park in her reserved spot. He then pulled in and parked by the next building.

Debbie juggled grocery bags and struggled with her keys as she walked toward a small courtyard with blooming flowers and colorful potted plants. As if he'd materialized from nowhere, Frank suddenly said, "Here, gimme," as he reached to take the bags from Debbie's arms.

"Jesus! Frank! What the hell?" She jumped. "Now you're followin' me?"

"Look, I just need a minute. Please. It's important." Frank followed Debbie inside her apartment without an invitation. She flipped on the lights, and Frank saw that they were surrounded by soft pink shades and feminine furnishings. He looked around and took it all in. He'd had no idea that there were so many shades of pink, but he had to admit that Debbie had done a great job with her cute apartment.

"You always wanted—oh, what's it called?" Frank said as he waved at the floral upholstered chair and ottoman in the living room.

"Mauve," Debbie said. "I always wanted to use mauve in my house."

"Huh. Well, it's nice."

As she unpacked her groceries, Debbie said, "So, what's so important, Frank?"

He walked over and looked at her. "I want you to come home."

She sighed as she put away a box of healthy-looking cereal. "Is *that* what you want? Or do you just not want to be alone?"

"Look, if I did things to upset you, I'm sorry. I'll work on it, I swear," Frank said as he picked up a box of couscous. "What *is* this shit?"

But she didn't answer as she took the box from him and put it in her pantry.

"For better or worse, Debbie. That's what we said," Frank went on.

"Except it never gets better, Frank. It's always more of the same, and I'm sick of it."

Frank inhaled deeply as he searched for the right words. But he'd barely slept in weeks and felt like he was drowning in family problems.

"You remember that doctor you talked about? What's that name—Minimoto? Montezuma?" Frank said.

"Matamoros," Debbie corrected. "Doctor Matamoros."

"Right. Well, I was thinkin' maybe we could go and see what he's got to say."

"*She.*"

"Oh, well, yeah, okay. We'll see what she's got to say, and maybe we can get the train back on the tracks. You know?" Frank looked for a reaction, but Debbie didn't seem to be softening.

She shook her head as she looked down at her countertop. "Frank, I asked you to go with me five years ago."

"Okay. And I'm admittin' you were right. C'mon, Debbie. Gimme a break. I'm tryin' here."

Debbie took the plastic lid off a can of coffee and tried to pull back the silver tab. But it tore off in her hand.

"Shit," she said as she reached for steak knife in a nearby butcher block.

"Wait. You just gotta pry up," Frank began as he moved to help her.

But Debbie stabbed the knife through the silver seal, twisted it, and then pulled back all at once. She held up the seal like a trophy and put the coffee beside the coffee maker on the counter.

Frank backed off, humbled that he wasn't needed.

"Smells good," he said. "What kind is it?"

"Hazelnut mocha."

"Hazel-what?" He scrunched up his face. "It's like I don't recognize you anymore. But I'll never forget the first time I saw you in ninth grade. You had that sexy Peggy Lipton hair, like on *Mod Squad*. You looked just like her."

Debbie pulled a pot from a cabinet and put it on the stovetop. "Yeah. Peggy Lipton was gorgeous," she remembered.

"*You* were gorgeous," Frank corrected. "Sittin' there at White Castle with Sue Sykora and Mary Ann DiBello. I couldn't stop starin' at you. Next thing I know, I hear myself sayin, right out loud—"

"That's the girl I'm gonna marry," Debbie and Frank said in unison.

"Yeah, I know," Debbie added sarcastically. "And

congratulations. You did that. But things change, Frank."

"Maybe they can change back," he said hopefully as he studied for any sign that she was softening.

"Look, Frank. This is what I do now. I come home from work. I make some couscous and a nice salad. I drink a glass of Chardonnay. I listen to whatever music I want—as long it's not Sinatra. I read a book, sometimes a magazine. And then I get to be happy and content."

Frank swallowed his pride as he crossed his arms over his chest, almost hugging himself in consolation. "So? This is it, then? You're not comin' home?"

With her back to him, Debbie shook her head.

Frank turned toward the door and walked out, his heart in his throat and tears in his eyes. As he walked to his truck, his legs felt like lead-weighted tree trunks, and his shoulders felt heavy with the weight of the world.

Debbie waited to hear her front door close. Then, she turned around and cried for all she was worth. She cried for Frank, for herself, for the two of them, and for Paul. Surrounded by cheerful shades of pink, Debbie cried for all of them.

CHAPTER 16

Frank turned his truck into his driveway. He dreaded going into his house since he knew that Debbie might never live with him again. Defeated and exhausted, Frank walked toward his front door. But just as he reached for the doorknob to insert his key, Frank thought better of it. He looked next door and then walked over to his parents' home instead.

"Aye, Dad," he said as he let himself in the back door and found Johnny eating a Swanson frozen dinner and reading the sports page. Johnny nodded at him while he chewed as Frank pulled up a chair at the kitchen table.

"Debbie just told me we're done."

"What d'ya want me to do about it?" Johnny asked.

"What's wrong with us, Dad?"

"Us? You mean, what's wrong with *you?*"

Frank shook his head to try and make sense of it all.

"You're sittin' here eatin' shit from a plastic tray, and I'm sleepin' alone. I'd say that *we* got the same fuckin' problem," Frank clarified.

"Yeah?" Johnny said with a mouth full of processed mashed potatoes. "And what's that?"

"The problem is we don't know how to love. The way you treated Ma, I did the same to Debbie. You can't love, so I can't either. We're both fucked."

Johnny suddenly reached across the table and grabbed Frank by the arm. Frank leaned back reflexively, but Johnny didn't let go.

"Don't you ever tell me that *I* don't know how to *love!*" Johnny said through clenched teeth.

"Really? Well, you sure know how to show it," Frank sarcastically shot back.

Johnny stared into his son's eyes, and then finally let go of Frank's arm, stood up, collected his thoughts and walked out of the kitchen without uttering another word. Frank put his head in his hands and regretted coming by. A few minutes later, he heard Johnny's truck drive off.

*

The home health aide carefully spooned soup into Mama D's mouth as Johnny leaned on Mama's kitchen counter and stared at the collage on her refrigerator. Rose smiled back at him, forever locked in time in the last photo taken of her at the church. Johnny recalled how in love they'd been, and how eager he and Rose were to start their life together. Being her husband was all he had ever wanted or needed.

Johnny wondered over the years how he could still be alive, since Rose had taken a piece of his heart with her. But then, one day, while down in his basement, he realized the reason he could still breathe was that he held a piece of Rose's heart, too. As he stared at the beautiful, smiling bride, he ached to hold her just one more time.

"Johnny," Mama D said. "Basta! You make'a you self a'crazy. You make'a me pazzo, too!"

"And on down the line," Betty, the aide, added as she rolled her eyes and dabbed the corner of Mama's mouth with a napkin.

"Pictures a'no change. People do," Mama D continued.

"I can't help it, Mama. I look around, and all I see is yesterday."

"Then Rosa taught'a you nothing," Mama said.

Johnny shook his head and walked out of the kitchen. He went and sat down in the living room, still surrounded by old memories and lost dreams. He thought back to a day in 1946 when he'd gone to see Rose at her home.

✶✶

A knockout brunette opened the door after Johnny knocked. She was cute, in her too-tight red angora sweater and pencil skirt. Her face was naturally pretty, like Rose's, but this woman oozed sensuality as if she were a gigantic billboard lit up on Broadway. Johnny's radar instantly went up to warn him that she could be trouble for a guy if he wasn't careful.

"Ohhh! Cute." She grinned, with red lips, as she looked Johnny up and down. "Lemme guess. Johnny, right? Well, don't just stand there, handsome. Come in."

She held the front door ajar, but only stepped back half a step. Johnny turned sideways, and he held his breath and tried not to brush against Connie's shapely sweater while he squeezed past her. Johnny looked more like he was doing the limbo than being invited inside.

The sultry brunette shut the door as she called upstairs, "Rose! Lover boy's here."

"Connie," she said when she turned her attention back to Johnny and extended her hand to shake his. "I'm Rose's cousin Connie."

Johnny shook her hand and said, "Funny, Rose never mentioned you before."

She laughed and said, "Well, I'm much older than Rosie. My family's from Manhattan, so we didn't really get out to Long Island much when I was growing up. Can I getcha somethin' to drink?"

"Oh, I don't—"

"You look like a bourbon man to me." Connie smiled as

she coquettishly cocked her head and looked up at Johnny.

Johnny nodded, impressed that she'd correctly read him.

"Comin' right up," Connie said as she disappeared into the kitchen.

Johnny heard her coming down the stairs before he saw Rose. She ran downstairs and straight into his arms to kiss him.

"You met my Cousin Connie?" she asked a moment later.

"You could say that, yeah."

"Isn't she just great?" Rose gushed. "She's from Manhattan. The Upper East Side. Connie's helping me plan the wedding! She's even been to Paris!"

"Paris? Really?" Johnny repeated.

"Mais oui, mon cherie," Connie chimed in as she returned with a pair of highball glasses and handed one to Johnny.

"Merci beaucoup," he smiled.

"Don't tell me. Normandy?" Connie asked as she eyed Johnny.

"Oui, oui, mademoiselle." Johnny held up his glass, and Connie clinked hers against it.

"Santé," she said, and then sipped her bourbon while studying Johnny over the rim of her glass. "So, turn around, soldier." Connie smiled as she twirled a pointed finger toward Johnny. "Let me get a good look at you."

From behind her, Rose motioned for Johnny to go and turn around. He felt awkward, but he obliged.

"Well now, aren't you just dreamy? Rose, you hit pay dirt!"

"*I* think so," Rose agreed.

"So, what'd you have in mind?" Connie asked Rose as they both continued to eye Johnny.

"I don't know. Top hat and tails, maybe?"

"And cover up the best parts?" Connie laughed as she leaned to view Johnny's backside.

"Uh, ladies?" Johnny interrupted. "Can I sit down now?"

"Oh! You're still here?" Connie asked. "Run along now and get your bride a tall one. This may take a while."

Connie picked up a large stack of bridal magazines from the entry table, and Rose followed her to the kitchen table. As soon as she sat down, Connie opened a magazine to a beautiful lace gown with a sweeping train.

"How about something like that?" she asked Rose.

"Wow! That's exquisite!" Rose gushed as she leaned in for a closer look.

Johnny didn't take his eyes off the giddy women at the table. He was intrigued by the unfamiliar banter, but he loved seeing Rose so excited as she and Connie flipped through the bridal magazine's pages.

"We're going to a bridal salon next week," Rose told Johnny as he watched from the doorway. "I can't wait to try on gowns!"

Johnny knew Mama D would be joining them when they went dress shopping. Mama was as excited as Johnny that he was marrying her Rosa. She already considered Johnny family and felt he was just like a son to her. Mama told them she had a feeling that life would be wonderful once the two young lovers had married.

A few days later, Rose floated into the bridal shop, elated that the day had finally come to try on gowns. Mama D took a seat in a white-and-gold brocade chair and waited while Rose and Connie looked through the endless sea of white gowns.

"Ma'am?" a suited salon employee asked Mama. "May I get you some champagne or perhaps some hot tea?"

"Tea would'a be nice." Mama smiled. "And'a bride need'a some chamomile if you have'a. Butterflies in'a da stomach, a'you know?"

"Oh, I know." The woman lightly laughed.

Rose and Connie handed gown after gown to a salon attendant, who whisked them into a large, mirrored dressing area in the back. Thirty minutes later, Rose went back to try on the dresses, and Mama moved to another chair in the dressing area.

The attendant held the first dress as Rose carefully stepped into it. Connie looked on as the dress easily zipped up the back and highlighted Rose's silhouette. Rose then tugged at the tulle and tried to adjust the satin bodice of the gown. Her heart raced and she'd begun to perspire. She felt light-headed, but Rose tried to ignore it and just enjoy the moment.

"Oh, Rosa! Che bella!" Mama gasped.

Rose grinned and looked in the mirror at Connie's reflection.

"Connie?" she asked.

"Like a million bucks!" Connie confirmed. "A million *before* taxes!"

"So many gowns'a!" Mama said. "Rosa, try'a one'a more. Let's a'see."

Rose tried on the next white gown, and the next, and the next after that. The dressing area suddenly felt small, and the air became heavy as the attendant tied the sash in the back of a gown she'd just buttoned for Rose.

"You don't like this one?" Rose asked Connie when she saw her cousin staring at her.

"Oh, no! It's perfect on you! Don't touch a thing. But I think you might need a teensy-tiny alteration," she said as she pulled a blue bottle from her handbag and gave it to Rose.

Rose looked questioningly at the bottle and then at her cousin as Mama walked back out to the main part of the salon to look at veils.

"Milk of magnesia, a.k.a. mother's milk, to all the top fashion models," Connie explained. "What? You think the models are all born that skinny?"

"Oh!" Rose realized what her cousin had meant. "Thanks, Connie. You're the best."

"It'll be our little secret," Connie said as she slipped the bottle into Rose's purse, which lay on a nearby settee.

Meanwhile, Johnny was in neighboring Far Rockaway, also preparing for their big day. As he walked out of Lamar Tuxedo, Johnny pushed a stick of gum into his mouth and turned down a nearby alley. After he'd passed a darkened doorway, Johnny suddenly felt a hard club or pipe at his neck, and he instinctively grabbed it and tried to break the chokehold it had on him.

"Where do you get the balls, Johnny? Not invitin' me to your wedding?" Kevin's voice said behind him as Johnny jerked away from his attacker.

"Get off me!" Johnny yelled as he spun around on Kevin.

"What'd I do? Huh? Just tell me," Kevin said as he held his nightstick.

"Maybe you looked after Rose just a little *too* good while I was gone," Johnny seethed.

"What? Did Rose say that?" Kevin looked shocked.

But Johnny didn't answer. He just continued. "I had my ass pinned down in mud and shit. Guys gettin' shot and blown up all over me, so you could stay home and bust jaywalkers. And that's the thanks I get?"

"Johnny, wait. I don't know where you got that crazy idea, but I swear—"

"If you weren't a cop, Kevin, I'd—"

"What, Johnny? You'd what? C'mon, lemme make it easy for you," Kevin yelled as he dropped his nightstick. "Take your best shot!"

"Go soak your head, you fuckin' traitor," Johnny spat.

BAM!

Kevin's fist slammed into Johnny's face.

POW!

Another fist drove full force into Johnny's gut.

Johnny stood tall and strong like an old redwood. Without a word, he touched his nose, looked at the blood on his fingers, then wiped it on Kevin's crisp uniform. As he walked away, Kevin stood seething in the alley.

Back in the bridal salon, Rose looked at her reflection in the trifold mirror and tried to believe that it was really her in the exquisite white gown. The bridal attendants had all stopped working with their other brides to admire Rose in her beautiful gown.

"Like a fairy princess," one woman said.

"I *feel* like a princess in a fairy tale," Rose beamed.

"And you're gonna get your Prince Charming and then live happily ever after," Connie said as she adjusted Rose's delicate beaded veil.

"I hope so."

"What is it, Rose?" Connie asked, surprised at Rose's comment.

"Aw, never mind. It's nothing."

"No, tell me," Connie urged.

"Well," Rose hesitated, "it's just that ever since Johnny

came home—"

"Woah." Connie put up her palms. "Listen, Rose, if you suspect the merchandise may be broken, you don't have to buy it."

"No, never mind. It's just jitters. Johnny's the one for me. I'm sure of it."

"Yes, he *is*!" Johnny's voice said as he walked toward the sound of Rose's voice in the dressing area.

"Johnny! Get out of here! It's bad luck! You can't see the gown before the wedding day!" Rose rushed toward the nearby alterations room to get out of his line of sight.

"You look unbelievable!" Johnny called behind her as she hurried away while holding up her dress.

"Now, Johnny! Out! I'm serious!" Rose said.

"You heard the lady," Connie said as she ushered Johnny back toward the front of salon. "And wipe that blood off your face. What's goin' on with you?"

Connie watched Johnny leave until he turned the corner. Mama D walked over and said, "Guess'a I should'a no tell Johnny we be'a here."

Even Mama D hadn't known that it had been Johnny who'd provided the money for Rose's gown, since Papa D had been ill and unable to work for some time. Papa D had tried not to accept Johnny's money, but his future son-in-law had insisted. "Listen, it's just some extra cash I won down at the pool hall. Let's put it to good use, and only you and me will ever know. You can help me out one day when I need it, okay?"

"You good'a boy, Johnny. My Rosa is'a lucky girl, and I'm a'grateful." Papa D squeezed Johnny's arm as he cleared his throat and fought back tears.

*

A week later, Johnny jogged up the steps to Rose's family's front door. He'd thought he was late as he started to knock on the door. But it flew open instead, and Connie reached for his hand and pulled him inside.

Connie seemed anxious and rushed as she walked him through the living room to the back of the quiet house. Johnny looked around but saw no one.

"Hey, where's Rose?" he asked.

"Oh, I sent her on an errand," Connie purred as she handed Johnny a glass of bourbon.

Johnny took the glass and watched as Connie walked in front of him. He was sure he'd never seen her swing her hips so dramatically, and he couldn't take his eyes off the vertical seam in the back of her tight skirt.

"She'll be gone for a while, but it'll give us time for one last fitting," Connie added. "Come on back, soldier."

"I thought all my alterations were done," he said. But Connie didn't answer.

Johnny knew the sewing room was back there, but he hesitated. Something just didn't feel right. But Johnny told himself it was just a sewing room, not a trap laid by the enemy. He walked back to the sewing room and entered the cluttered space. Without a word, Connie stepped in front of the door and then locked it.

The ominous click panicked Johnny, but before he could object, Connie used her body to push Johnny against the wall. Her mouth was on him and hungrily kissing him as Johnny tried to flatten himself to get away. There wasn't even room for air between them as Connie pressed her breasts into Johnny's chest. He struggled to get her off him, but when she reached down and grabbed his pants and squeezed, Johnny's body reacted without checking with him first. He reflexively moaned, and for a moment, his mouth started kissing her back, hot and heavy. Before he even knew he'd moved his arm, his hand was underneath Connie's tight sweater and exploring.

But Johnny's brain soon caught up with his body, and he pushed her away hard.

"No!" he yelled as Connie stumbled in her high heels but quickly caught herself on the sewing table.

Johnny was confused. He'd had combat training, and he knew for sure that he was in enemy territory. Yet unlike in war, decorum and manners had to be considered. And with family—and future family—involved, he knew he was in a precarious spot.

Connie was the one who was confused now. She seemed

rattled as she ran a hand through her hair, straightened her skirt, and then smoothed its front with her hands. Johnny forced himself to look away from her heaving cleavage as she bent over, and he wiped her lipstick off his lips.

"Listen, Connie," Johnny stammered. "I mean, um, you're a great-lookin' gal, and any guy would be crazy-lucky to have you between the sheets. But I love Rose, *I do*. I'm sorry."

Connie's face was bright red. Her eyes looked angry and hurt. But she finally cleared her throat, stood up straight, and said, "Nothin' to be sorry about, soldier. Just had to make sure you wouldn't be hurtin' my Rose."

"What?" Johnny gasped. "So, you mean, I passed the test?"

"Only if you're smart enough to keep your mouth shut," she said, without looking at him, as she unlocked the door and then held it open for Johnny to pass.

Confused more than ever, Johnny shook his head and walked through the doorway.

"Wait." He stopped walking and looked at Connie. "What if I hadn't stopped?"

Connie raised her eyebrow and grinned. "You'll never know, will you?" And with that, she gently pushed him all the way out of the sewing room.

Johnny went to find a mirror and check for lipstick. Connie shut the sewing room's door and then sat down at the sewing machine and tried to steady her shaking hands. She clasped her hands and closed her eyes. When she leaned her head back, a single tear ran down her flushed cheek.

*

CHAPTER 17

Frank's truck turned into the parking lot of the Nassau County Medical Center on two wheels. The police cruiser pulled in behind him, right on his rear bumper. But Frank kept driving until he found an open space. He parked his truck and jumped out, almost in one motion. The police car pulled behind, with its blue lights flashing, and blocked the pickup truck.

"Aw, shit! Frank! It's *you!* What the hell, man? Didn't you see my lights flashin' back here?" the uniformed officer said.

"Course I saw your fuckin' lights, Marco! But I knew it was you, and I'm in a hurry here!" Frank hollered, as he ran across the lawn of the medical building, leaped a short hedge, and darted into the lobby. Marco stood frozen in shock, with his mouth agape, as he watched until Frank was out of sight.

"Fuckin' Frankie!" he said, as he recalled that his dad, Marco Sr., had always had a hard spot when it came to Frank. "Just stay away from that whole family," Marco Sr. had told him. "I don't like Frankie or his father—Mista Perfection. Couldn't stand him in high school, can't stand him now. Somebody needs to knock him down to size." Marco wondered what his dad never liked about Johnny. He considered that his father had just been jealous of the guy. But he would never get to ask his father more about it, since Marco Sr. had died of a sudden illness years earlier.

As Marco turned off the flashing lights on his cruiser, Frank flew into Doctor Leitner's office.

"You found somethin', didn't you, Doc? I could tell from your voice on the phone! I got here as quick as I could!" Without being offered a seat, Frank sat down across from the doctor, whose desktop was covered with pages from Rose's coroner's report, along with countless handwritten notes.

"Okay," the doctor began, as he finished reading a page. "With the elevated levels of magnesium oxide in the blood, I'd expect the culprit would've been the citrate of magnesia. Apparently, she was trying to lose weight."

"Before her wedding, to fit into her dress." Frank nodded, in realization.

"Hmm, I see. But overuse leads to dehydration," the doctor went on, "and that lowers the electrolytes, leaving the heart susceptible to arrhythmia."

Frank leaned back and let the doctor go on.

"Maybe she was dehydrated from dieting. Couple that with the stress of getting married, and bingo! She drops dead of a heart attack."

"But no one mentioned anything about a heart attack," Frank said.

"Well, it wasn't on that first report you showed me, but that's what it says here," the doctor responded. "However, the curious thing is, they also list asphyxia. She apparently had a history of asthma or respiratory distress. But the question I have is why did she present with acute tracheobronchitis— you see, *that's* caused by some irritation or an irritant that's introduced into the respiratory system."

"I don't understand. So, you're sayin' there's a missing piece?" Frank said.

"No. I'm saying there's a piece *too many*," Doctor Leitner explained. "Most likely, theophylline, strongly contraindicated by the citrate of magnesia."

"C'mon! English, doc. What's the bottom line?" Frank impatiently urged.

"It appears that she may have been poisoned."

Frank sat back again, stunned and shocked. He tried to digest what he had just heard, but it made no sense to him. For the first time, Frank was speechless.

"And there's something else," the doctor added, as he cautiously tapped his pen at a highlighted sentence on one page of the coroner's report.

*

Frank jerked the steering wheel and whipped his truck onto the road as he left his meeting with the doctor. He'd expected answers, not more questions. He pounded his steering wheel as he pressed the gas harder, and the wind whipped through his truck, and through his thick hair, compliments of Johnny. Frank shifted anxiously as he sped toward home.

"Aw, shit. Are you fuckin' kiddin' me, Marco?" he yelled, as he looked in his rearview mirror at the blue flashing lights.

But he still didn't have time to stop. Frank had too much on his mind.

"Yeah? Fuck *you*, Marco!" Frank hollered as he pumped his middle finger out his window. "No wonder my dad couldn't stand your fuckin' father! Same reason I beat *your* ass in high school! You're all a buncha pains in the asses!"

"Pull your vehicle to the *side*, Frank!" Marco's voice blared from the loudspeaker on his cruiser.

"Blow it out your *ass*, Marco!"

After about eight miles, the lights turned off and so did Marco. He made a right at the next intersection and gave up on Frank. Besides, Marco had always felt bad for telling Frank that his mother wasn't his real mom when they were kids. That was also the reason Marco had felt he had a beating coming when Frank whipped him at school one day.

*

Frank sat on the back concrete steps at his parents' home. He was deep in thought as he went over what Doctor Leitner had told him. Frank sighed and remembered when his biggest concern was what his dad did in his basement.

Johnny was opening the back door to walk outside but paused when he saw Frank. After a second, he continued down the steps, without a word, and across the lawn to a compost heap. Johnny pulled the shovel out of the heap and then began silently shoveling compost into a nearby red wheelbarrow. He was older but still in good shape. Frank watched his dad's biceps and forearms flex with each shovelful.

For more than five minutes, neither father nor son said a word.

Finally, Frank spoke. "One time, I'll never forget, I stayed home sick from school. Ma had to go out that afternoon, so you came home early from work to be with me. I guess I must'a been pretty sick 'cause you let me watch cartoons on the couch in my pajamas."

With his back to Frank, Johnny slowed his shoveling and listened. He swallowed hard and shut his eyes and sighed. Johnny didn't turn around to meet his son's eyes as Frank continued.

"You asked me if I wanted a sandwich," he said. "I wasn't hungry. In fact, I felt kinda queasy, but I couldn't say no. So, I watched you get some cold cuts from the fridge. And I watched as you got out the bread and then sprinkled oil on one side and vinegar on the other. Then you got out the lettuce, but you pulled out the bad pieces and only used the good ones. And you put some meat on the bread, along with some white cheese of some sort. Then I watched you close the sandwich, position Ma's big bread knife at one corner of the crust, and slice diagonally to the opposite corner—like you were makin' it all classy or somethin'."

Frank grinned at the memory.

"You had pressed too hard, and you'd put your thumb right through the top slice of bread. But you didn't think I was watching, so you quickly flipped the sandwich over, so it'd look perfect when you brought it to me with chips and a glass of milk. And I remember lifting up the sandwich and seeing your big thumbprint in the bread, like proof you'd made it. All I could think was, 'Wow. My old man just made me a sandwich.'"

Johnny stopped shoveling and stood up straight as Frank's words hung in the air between them. Frank got up from the step, brushed off his pants, and then laid the coroner's report on the step.

"Dad, she was poisoned," he said.

Johnny's shoulders lifted and then fell heavily, but he still didn't turn around.

"I'm really sorry," Frank added as he turned to go into the house, unsure of what to do next. He glanced at the basement door when he walked in but kept walking past it and went to get a beer from the refrigerator.

Johnny stared at the folder on the step. His jaw clenched and so did his fists, but he couldn't make himself move closer and pick it up. Frank's words had hit him with a one-two punch, and he still felt winded and unable to catch his breath. The house phone started to ring inside, but Johnny stood frozen. It continued to ring without stopping. Johnny figured Frank must've gone out the front door and walked over to his house. He stomped toward the house and up the steps, snatching up the folder on the way to answer his insistent phone.

"Hello?"

"Yeah."

"Aw, Jesus," he finally gasped as he shut his eyes and ran his hand through his hair.

*

There were so many people, lots who'd known the family since they moved from Rosedale, and even a few who had come from Rosedale. Mama DeFabrizio looked peaceful as she lay amid the white satin lining of her coffin. Her delicate fingers held her rosary beads, and her head rested on a white satin and lace pillow.

Johnny's legs felt leaden and heavy, like they wouldn't work right. Each step was more difficult than the last, as he walked up the aisle toward the casket and all the flowers that surrounded it. He'd have preferred to be facing a firing squad. It would have been easier.

When he finally got to the casket, Johnny knelt before the woman who had been a mother to him. He prayed the Lord's Prayer as his shoulders heaved and shook uncontrollably. He'd lost so much, and it all had ended in that place, in Morelli's Funeral Home. He and Rose were to be married, but instead of a wedding, her funeral was held. Rose was laid to rest in her wedding dress, forever immortalized in the gown she'd wanted to wear on her special day when she had planned to begin her life with Johnny.

They'd also held Celia's wake at the same place in 1983. The funeral home had overflowed into the parking lot with people. They had all shown up to pay their respects to kindhearted Celia, the eternally smiling young woman who had never matured past her childhood innocence, and who had loved everyone she had ever met. Even Papa D had ended his days in this life with a wake at Morelli's. Everyone who attended a wake at Morelli's knew he'd also end up there one day. Even Charles Morelli, founder of the funeral home, had made his last appearance there at his own wake. For those who lived in Inwood, there were some things that were guaranteed in this life: death, taxes, and a wake at Morelli's.

But now it was time to let Mama D go, and Johnny wished to be anywhere else than saying goodbye to her. He sobbed as he thought of never seeing her again. The pain was almost too much to bear.

Suddenly, a comforting hand touched Johnny's shaking back. He tried to get ahold of himself as he looked up to see Betty, the home health aide who had cared for Mama D for years. Johnny couldn't speak, but he nodded at Betty as he turned around and headed back up the aisle. But after just a few steps, he stopped.

"What're you doin' here?" he asked Lena.

"Came to pay my respects."

Johnny looked around at all the people. "Come outside," he told her.

"No." Lena pushed past him to make her way down the aisle.

"C'mon. Don't make me make a scene here."

"John, that's entirely up to you. I don't care what you do." She kept walking, and so did he.

"Why are you doin' this, and today, of all days?" he asked, as they got to Mama's casket.

Lena made the cross sign in front of herself and then knelt before Mama to talk to her for the last time.

"You were such a nice lady, and a good person. And I understand. I do. But you've had him long enough. Can you please let him go now?"

Johnny leaned down and whispered, "Okay, you sound like a loon. Let's go."

"Stop it." Lena shook his arm off. "Even in wood, in

death, she gets more than me."

"You got everything you wanted. What're you sayin?" Johnny pleaded.

Lena stood up and turned to face him as they moved off to the side to allow others time with Mama. But Johnny could tell Lena was fuming.

"*I* got everything I wanted?" Lena mocked. "No, John. I'll tell you what *I* got! I got the moods. I got the temper. I got the yelling. I got all the negative crap nobody else ever saw outta perfect Johnny Mastantuono! They got the cake and even the frosting, and all I ever got was the forgotten crumbs! All the love and care, and all the kindness went to her and her dead daughter! When I ran to that house and called an ambulance that day, I had no idea it was for the woman who held your heart—and whose memory you'd never let go of, not ever! What the *hell*, John?"

"That's enough!" Johnny said as he grabbed Lena's elbow and hustled her toward the back of the funeral home so they wouldn't be a spectacle. All eyes were on them as they made their exit, still bickering in strained, hushed tones, but with dramatic gestures and expressions.

Frank's truck turned into a nearby parking spot in the lot, and he heard them before he saw them. That telltale bickering could be none other than his parents.

"Did you ever, even once, hold my hand on the beach, John?" Ma angrily asked. "Or did you ever make me breakfast on a Sunday morning, or just bring me coffee, just once?"

Johnny had no answers, but he said, "I will not stand here and be accused like this—"

"Because you don't have a leg to stand on, John! You know I'm right!"

Johnny waved her off in disgust and then turned back toward the funeral home. "I'm goin' back inside," he said.

"Well, of course you are! She's your family, John! I'm just the moron who cooked your food, washed your clothes, and put up with your shit for the last fifty years!"

Johnny stopped walking and turned back toward Lena. Frank instinctively rushed to get between them.

"Okay, you two, enough. Knock it off."

"Don't look at me like that!" Johnny told Lena, without acknowledging Frank. "Wipe that look off'a your face!"

But she wouldn't back off. "Do you love me, John? Did you *ever* even love me?"

Without a word, Johnny threw up his hands in defeat and angrily stomped back toward the building. He knew there was no reasoning with her.

"I married a dead man!" Lena yelled toward Johnny's back. "You're as dead as she is! And you know what? *I'm alive*, John! Damn you!"

Frank stood in front of her, unsure of what to do but quite sure he needed to contain his volatile mother as onlookers watched the unfolding scene in the parking lot.

"C'mon, Ma," he said as he led her in tears to his truck. "Let's go over here."

Johnny went back inside the funeral home and took a seat. Tears ran down his weathered face as he held one hand with the other to try and stop the shaking. But he wasn't just crying for Mama D. It was everything. The last few days had seemed surreal. Since he had gotten the call about Mama only minutes after Frank had given him the coroner's findings, Johnny hadn't been able to process what he had learned about Rose. He cried harder and harder, but it never washed away all his pain, not ever. None of it was fair. None of it made sense.

Johnny's mind raced as he considered the possibilities of what could have happened on that day, the day that had forever changed his life's path. He'd never mentioned to Rose her cousin's seduction attempt after Connie had made a pass at him in the sewing room. It hadn't seemed necessary, since Connie had made a quick exit.

**

Connie couldn't leave fast enough that day, as she wrapped a French silk scarf around her neck and threw one end over the shoulder of her Chanel blazer.

"I can't believe you can't stay for the wedding," Rose said. "I'll miss you being here."

"Well, that's the life of a busy career girl, I suppose. Besides, my work here is done." Connie smiled nervously as she slid into the waiting taxicab and then slipped on her oversize sunglasses. "Oh, and here, Rose." She handed a blue bottle to her cousin through the cab's open window. "Now, don't ease up. You look swell, but just in case, I left you another secret weapon underneath your bed. Brought it all the way from Gimbels."

"Gimbels? Wow! Connie, how can I ever thank you enough for all you've done?" Rose leaned in the cab's rear window for a last hug. She couldn't see that Connie wasn't smiling, not in the slightest. But when Rose stepped back, Connie shot her a toothy, practiced pageant contestant smile and waved goodbye with a slender, gloved hand.

"East Seventy-Ninth, Manhattan," she told the cab driver as she settled against the back seat.

*

CHAPTER 18

Johnny slipped off his suit jacket and threw it in the passenger seat. Then he got behind the steering wheel and loosened his necktie and took it off, and then he unbuttoned the top two shirt buttons. He started driving but unbuttoned the cuffs of his shirt and rolled up the sleeves to the elbows as he steered with his knee through the rainy night. The sky had threatened to open up all evening, but the rain poured so heavily now that Johnny's truck's wiper blades couldn't keep up, not even on the highest setting.

Johnny parked as close to the door as possible, but he had no choice but to make a run for it, with no umbrella in his truck. He shook his head when he realized Lena would have grabbed an umbrella earlier since it had looked like rain. In fact, he remembered, Lena had carried a compact umbrella at

Morelli's. She was always prepared like that, he recalled. It was always Lena who had reminded Johnny to take his medicine. It was Lena who had handled the Christmas shopping, the holiday meals, and even the Santa Claus touches that Frank had loved as a kid. It had been Lena who'd made sure to remind Johnny when Frank had an event or a game. It was Lena who had spent time getting to know Frank's friends and his girlfriends.

Although he was seventy-five, Johnny ran through the puddles in his good leather shoes until he got to the awning in front of Willow Tavern. He'd walked toward the tavern a thousand times over the years.

"Couldn't dodge those raindrops, huh?" a young guy joked as he lit a cigarette for his girlfriend.

But John was in no mood for useless banter. He went inside the tavern and made a beeline for the bar. Mike, the regular bartender, was busy at the cash register on the other side of the bar. Johnny had seen Mike look over at him, but not move closer.

SLAP!

Johnny smacked the bar top impatiently, and Mike looked over at him. He instantly realized Johnny was in a mood.

"What?" Mike asked from about ten feet away as he ran a report on the register.

"Bourbon," Johnny said. "Double. No, triple."

Mike eyed Johnny as he poured the bourbon, filling the

glass to the rim. "Knock yourself out. Literally," Mike said.

Johnny first sipped it, and then tossed back the whole glass, first gulping, and then nearly gagging, as he drained every drop of whiskey. He replaced the glass on the bar and wiped a hand over his mouth. His body shuddered as heat spread through his insides like an out-of-control wildfire that would burn everything in its path.

The clacking and popping sounds of pool balls got Johnny's attention, and he turned away from the bar. He moved through the crowd as the bourbon relaxed him a bit. Johnny had hoped the bourbon would make him forget, even for a little a while.

But as he pushed through the men and women, his mind went back decades, to a time when they were all so much younger. Johnny tried physically to ignore the feelings and shake off memories of himself and his younger friends as he made his way to the men's room. Suddenly, he noticed the last booth along the wall. In it, Kevin McCarthy argued with someone Johnny couldn't see. But Johnny moved a few feet to get a better look. It was Gina who sat across from Kevin. Johnny seethed with anger as he watched his sister wag an accusatory finger at Kevin, who then appeared to defend himself, based on his body language and facial expression.

As Johnny thought of all the ways he'd like to rip Kevin apart, he watched as Kevin took Gina's hand, kissed her palm, and then pressed it to his cheek. Gina reached over and stroked Kevin's face and then leaned across the table to kiss him on the lips. Johnny's eyes filled with rage mixed with utter confusion as he spun around and got out of there.

"Whole fuckin' world's gone crazy," Johnny muttered. And then he recalled the morning in 1946 when a group of women had sat around Mama D's table, making sandwiches in a mini assembly line, and one of them had said that same thing—or almost that same thing. They'd been talking about the war and its effects on soldiers, and one woman said, "The world's gone crazy."

**

"We no a'care about the world!" Mama D had said. "We a'care about the wedding day! Now, who can a'help to iron a'some a'dresses?"

There were three ironing boards set up in Mama's living room and kitchen. Ladies ironed wedding clothes while men busted open ice bags and dumped cubes and blocks into plastic-lined bins and ice chests, occasionally stopping to sample the beer to make sure it was adequate for the wedding celebration, yet careful not to let Mama see. Girls in white silk slips and hair curlers ran around frantically looking for makeup and hairspray.

"Did'a Rosa eat?" Mama asked no one in particular. No one answered since everyone was preoccupied. "That'a girl of mine has no eat'a in days. She a tiny. It's a'crazy, like'a this world!"

"Johnny!" Mama said. "Why'a you here? Home! Go a'home and get'a dressed! You done enough! You no see the bride! Its'a bad a'luck! Now, a'go! A'go!"

Celia rushed in and went to Gina, who was putting clear polish on her nails. "Can I see the dress yet, Gina?" she asked hopefully. "Please, can I?"

"Soon. Very soon," she told her sister. "Mama, where's Vinny?"

"You tell'a me! I'm a'still a'waiting for my a'wine!" Mama complained. "I sent'a him to get'a the a'wine, but a'he should'a been a'back by now."

Gina looked at the clock on the wall. "He's gotta get Johnny to the church, too."

Mama rolled her eyes and then made the cross against herself, as if it were a last desperate resort that might hurry Vinny along.

"Is that Gina down there I hear?" Rose called as she leaned over the stair banister in her curlers, wearing a light pink bathrobe. "I need Gina. Right now. And alone."

Gina closed the bottle of nail polish, blew on her fingernails, and obediently headed straight upstairs. Celia started to follow her sister, but Mama reached out and stopped her.

"In'a kitchen," she directed Celia. "Come'a now."

"But I want to help Rose, too," Celia protested.

"You will'a be a'help. We need a hand in'a kitchen. Come,

I a'show you," Mama said as she steered Celia into the kitchen.

Upstairs, Rose's bedroom door flew open, and Gina rushed inside, still blowing on her fingernails. The beautiful wedding dress hung on Rose's closet door. But Rose looked concerned and stressed, and very pale, as she took yet another swig from the blue bottle her cousin Connie had left her. She then took out the rest of her hair curlers and tossed them onto her dressing table.

"You want me to get you some water?" Gina asked her. "You look pale, like it might be more than wedding-day jitters."

"No, what I want is to fit into my dress. You've gotta help me," Rose pleaded as she bent down to pull a fancy-looking box from beneath her bed. Gina watched curiously as Rose opened the department store box and pulled aside the perfumed tissue paper.

"A corset?" Gina said as she scrunched up her nose at what appeared to be a medieval torture device with all its metal hooks and lacing. "You don't need that!"

"Not just any corset," Rose corrected. "This is a really nice one from Gimbels. It's paper-thin and very expensive. It should work, and no will ever know I'm even wearing it."

"How'd you get your hands on that?" Gina asked.

"I've got my sources. Now, come on and help me get into this thing. I want to look perfect for Johnny."

"Pa-leeez. You could wear a burlap sack and Johnny would still only have eyes for you, Rose."

Rose faced the window and held her loose hair off her shoulders with both hands. The rest of her hair was in curlers atop her head as Gina reached around with the corset and then began to hook it in back.

"This does not look the least bit comfortable," Gina said as she pulled the fabric sides together, a bit at a time, and hooked each eye, one at a time. "I thought they'd outlawed these horrific torture devices, along with chastity belts."

"Don't make me laugh," Rose joked. "This thing is far too tight for me to laugh. The best I can do is smile—but never exhale."

"Oh, I don't believe that for a minute! You'll be laughing and smiling soon, and you'll be the most beautiful bride!"

"I'll just wait to breathe again until after I say, 'I do,'" Rose said as she sucked in her already flat stomach as Gina pulled the corset even tighter.

"More. Go tighter," Rose said. "I feel like I've gained a few pounds since the final fitting."

"I don't see how. You never eat. In fact, Mama was asking if you've eaten anything today."

"I'll eat *and* breathe *after* the wedding," Rose said. The corset pinched even tighter as Gina connected the final hook.

"I'm not sure you need to lace this thing all the way," Gina began.

"Do it. As tight as it'll go. It's just for a few hours. Go ahead," Rose urged as she drew in a deeper breath.

When she was done lacing the corset and cinching it, Gina took the gown from its padded satin hanger and helped Rose to step into it. Rose put her hands on either side of her waist as Gina zipped the dress. But it didn't zip smoothly.

"See? I *have* gained weight!" Rose cringed.

"No, it's just this zipper," Gina said. "I can get it. It'll go. Hang on."

"I'm sucking in as much as I can," Rose said.

"There! Got it!" Gina stood back and looked at Rose's reflection in her floor-length mirror. "Beautiful! Just beautiful!"

Mama appeared in the doorway wearing the mother-of-the-bride dress Rose had selected especially for her. Speechless, she covered her mouth with her hands as tears filled her eyes. "Mia Rosa," she whispered. "Bella! Perfecto!"

"Mama! Mama!" someone yelled up the stairs. "There's a problem in the kitchen! We need you!"

"What'a now?" Mama said as she threw her hands up and went to see what the latest emergency could possibly be. "Rosa, the limo be here a'soon!"

Gina and another bridesmaid fanned Rose with magazines to help cool her, while another girl rushed in with a tabletop oscillating fan and plugged it in.

"Ahh, thank you." Rose sighed. "Maybe I *will* take a drink

of water."

As the girls tried to keep Rose cool, Mama shrieked downstairs. "The wine a'no here! The egg'a biscuits too dry! And now'a the limo is a'late! What'a next?"

"What else can go wrong?" Rose said. "My nerves are shot!"

"I can help!" Celia said cheerfully as she glided into Rose's bedroom, beaming from ear to ear, proudly wearing her bridesmaid's dress.

"Celia, Rose is very busy right now," Gina said.

"No, it's fine. You do whatever you want, honey." Rose smiled at Celia.

"I have nerves, too, Rose," Celia said. "I know what it's like."

"I remember," Rose said. "We share that, don't we?"

"Yep!" Celia grinned. "We share Johnny, and we share nerves!"

Suddenly, the front door flew open downstairs. Papa D lugged a case of wine, with Vinny following behind with another case.

"The limo is a'waiting out'aside!" Papa D yelled to everyone in the house.

"Finally!" Mama yelled. "Let's a'go, girls! Everyone a'get out. Go!"

"You heard the general," Gina laughed as she straightened Rose's pearls.

"Who is the general?" Celia looked confused as she happily bounded downstairs in front of Rose.

The bridesmaids checked their hair and makeup one last time in the mirror above the entry table, and then they hurried outside to the waiting limo.

"Oh! I almost forgot!" Rose said as she lifted her dress, turned around, and ran back upstairs.

Papa D plucked an egg biscuit from a tray in the kitchen and took a bite. He chewed twice, made a face, and then spit it out into the trash can and got some water. Rose rushed back down the stairs and nearly bumped into her dad.

"Bella, Rosa!" he called after her as she rushed out the door. "I'm a right'a behind you!"

"Thank you, Papa!"

As she hurried outside, Gina was chastising Vinny. "Go! You need to get Johnny and get him to the church! You shoulda picked him up already! I don't know what you've been doin' all this time! Hurry it up, Vinny!"

The girls helped Rose into the limo and then straightened her gown, so it didn't wrinkle. "She's so hot. She's sweltering," Gina said as she dabbed Rose's sweating upper lip with a lace handkerchief. "Look at her face. It must be that —"

"Dress!" Rose interjected as she looked wide-eyed at Gina and warned her soon-to-be sister-in-law to keep quiet about the corset. "It's the *dress*, that's all."

"Vito!" Mama said as she cranked open the window closest to her. "Open'a window for Rosa! She a'hot!"

Gina fanned Rose's face with her hand, for what it was worth, as the limo driver steered toward the church. Rose couldn't wait to see Johnny. All her dreams were coming true. She just wished she felt better.

"It's just nerves," Celia told Rose. "But they'll go away. I know they will. I'm sure of it."

Rose smiled at sweet Celia. Her innocence was refreshing and reminiscent of what was important in life. Rose knew why Celia was so special to Johnny, and she loved that he adored his older sister. Since they'd lost their parents, Johnny had been both brother and father to Celia. Like everyone else, Johnny never minded when it came to Celia, and he always looked out for his sister.

*

"Yep. Whole world's gone crazy," Johnny slurred as he turned into his driveway too fast and sheared off the side of his mailbox. "Aw, shit," he groaned when he got out and surveyed the damage.

Johnny forced himself to stop thinking of the awful day his world had changed forever. The wedding day, and his monumental loss, had been on his mind since Mama D had just left him. It felt like everyone he ever loved ultimately left him.

Somehow, losing Mama made Rose seem even further

away. For as long as Mama had been alive, a little bit of Rose lived on in her mother's memories. Johnny and Mama had always shared a deep love for Rose, so they understood each other's pain, even without talking about it. There wasn't another soul alive who'd ever understand his pain and loss now.

Johnny walked into his dark, quiet house and tossed his keys on the table. It had been another emotional day, and it had taken a toll on Johnny. But he knew he wouldn't be able to sleep. Even after all he'd had to drink, coupled with emotional exhaustion, sleep wouldn't come. He was sure of it.

"Maybe just one more," he thought as he fumbled with the lock on his liquor cabinet. He tried again and again to insert his key into the small lock, but he couldn't focus long enough to line up the key. Frustrated, he kicked in the glass and reached in and pulled out a bottle. "Put it on the list!" he mumbled. "I'll fix it right after I put in a new mailbox."

Still damp from the earlier rain, Johnny sat down in the kitchen and drank straight from the bottle. He snickered to himself that no one could tell him to go and get a glass or to stop drinking and that he'd already had enough. But the truth was that he missed having Lena do those things. Johnny took a big swig from the bottle as he eyed the basement door.

He'd grown tired and bewildered. Nothing felt right, and Johnny doubted it ever would again. Even he had grown weary with his daily basement ritual, and he knew it wasn't healthy. But he couldn't stop, or else he feared he'd forget Rose and lose the loved they'd shared. Going into the basement and spending time with their memories had kept her alive for him over the decades. But he'd screwed up everything, and he knew he was out of chances.

"One more time," he whispered as he got up and went to the basement door. Johnny struggled to maintain his balance on the wooden steps as he carried his bottle downstairs. As he opened the workroom's door, Johnny knew it was the last time. He went in and immediately pulled out the footlocker. He tried to focus on the contents as he pulled out his old uniform, a canteen, helmet linings, and a box of vintage ammo. He reached in and pulled out a black-and-white photo of Rose and held it to his chest against his heart as he sobbed.

When he replaced the photo in the footlocker, he saw the gun he'd stored in the bottom. It was a WWI German Luger. Johnny picked it up and looked at it. He squatted before the box of memories but lost his balance and fell backward against a wall. The box of ammo was within his reach. He picked it up and emptied all the bullets onto the floor. As he handled the Luger, he picked up a bullet and stared at it for a minute. Then he shakily loaded it into the Luger's chamber with trembling fingers. He stared at the loaded gun and took a few more sips from his bottle.

Bits and pieces flooded back to him as ghosts of the past revisited Johnny. Fragments of conversations and flashes of memories taunted him. He couldn't stop them, not any of them.

"I married a dead man! You're as dead as she is!" Lena's voice screamed inside his head.

"Kevin's taking *real good* care of Rose," Vinny's letter had read.

"We'll be together for all eternity." Rose smiled in his memory.

"*She's* your family!" Lena yelled.

"You got'a respect a'girl before you can'a love her!" Mama D said.

"Rose is so nice!" Celia grinned. "And pretty, too!"

"What about me, Johnny?" Gina asked. "What am I supposed to do?"

"Sorry I'm late," Vinny said, "but I'll have you to the church on time!"

"Wow. My dad made me a sandwich," Frank said.

Johnny couldn't stop the rapid-fire memories and cacophony in his head. So, he took another drink, and then another one, in attempt to drown the voices and silence them. But they wouldn't stop. Johnny hung his head in his old, wrinkled hands as the workshop swayed around him.

He finally slowly stood up, falling slightly forward, but then leaning back to catch himself and recover his balance.

"You got this. Okay. Go slow," he silently coached himself.

Then, Johnny took another drink, as if that would help him find clarity and keep his balance. But he didn't go back upstairs. Instead, he walked outside and into the night. The rain had stopped, but the ground was soaked. The chirping crickets seemed louder than usual to Johnny as he walked toward the street, carrying his bottle and the old Luger.

The street was quiet. It was late, and none of the neighbors had their lights on as Johnny walked toward Gina's house. He stumbled up his sister's driveway and noticed Kevin's car was parked in the back. Johnny fumed as he took another drink and walked to the front door. He'd always wondered if Kevin had something to do with the fateful October day that forever altered his life. Johnny had even contemplated whether Vinny had withheld details from him. But when he'd married Gina, Johnny had decided to let it go. But that was a long time ago, and Vinny had been gone for years.

"Ayyy!" he hollered as he banged on Gina's front door with a force that would wake the dead. "Gina! Ayyy! Open up! I know you're in there!"

A light went on upstairs, and then Johnny heard footsteps inside. Suddenly, Gina jerked her front door open as she tied her bathrobe and squinted at Johnny.

"Johnny! What the hell is wrong you? Do you know what time it is?"

"Just get his ass out here. Right now," Johnny slurred as he tried to focus on Gina—or, at least, on *one* of Gina.

"You're drunk. Go home, Johnny."

"Or what?" he snickered. "You'll call the *cops*? You're sleepin' with one of their finest, right?"

Just then, the door opened wider, and Kevin stood in a T-shirt and boxers beside Gina. Johnny's jaw tightened, and he glared hatefully at Kevin.

"You knew. You sonofabitch, you knew! All this time, you knew!" Johnny told him.

"Knew *what*?" Kevin asked.

"Don't you play dumb with me!" Johnny yelled.

"What's he talkin' about?" Gina asked Kevin.

"Like *you* don't know!" Johnny said to Gina. "She was like a sista to you!"

"Johnny, you're not makin' any—"

"She was poisoned!" Johnny wailed. "My Rosie was *poisoned* on our wedding day! All these years! All these fuckin' years, I wondered!"

Gina looked at Kevin in horror as Johnny continued his rant on her doorstep.

"They couldn't figure it out back then," Johnny said to Kevin. "But you knew they would one day. You knew someone would figure it out! You either did it, or you covered it up!"

"You're talking nonsense. Go home and sleep it off,

Johnny," Kevin said as he moved to shut the door.

"Don't you fuckin' move!" Johnny said as he pulled the Luger from his pocket and tried to steady himself as he shut one eye and focused on the wavy images in front of him.

CHAPTER 19

As the limo pulled up outside Our Lady of Good Counsel, church bells rang, and cars and onlookers were everywhere. Family and friends chatted happily as they filed into the church while organ music filled the air. Rose took small breaths and tried to steady her nerves.

Inside the church's cloak room, Vinny adjusted Johnny's tie. "I told ya I'd get you here on time, didn't I? What're friends for, right?"

Suddenly, Kevin McCarthy appeared in the doorway in his police uniform. Johnny's eyes instantly went cold with hatred.

"What're *you* doin' here, Kevin?" he spat in disgust.

"I got put on crowd control."

"Yeah? Control this!" Vinny smirked as he slammed the door in Kevin's face.

On the other side of the church, Rose's bridesmaids surrounded her in a flurry of last-minute makeup retouching and primping. She was hot and uncomfortable but determined to enjoy her moment with Johnny.

"Rose?" Gina said. "What is it? What's wrong?"

Rose's face was red, and she didn't look well.

"It feels like it's getting tighter," Rose said as she moved awkwardly and tried to adjust the bodice of her dress.

"What? No, it can't be. If anything, it'd relax some and get looser. Just try and relax," Gina said as she fanned the bride.

"I am. Really, I am."

"Everyone! Places! Places, everyone! It's a'time!" Mama D called out.

*

Lena heard something outside her bedroom window. She got out of bed and walked to the window to try and figure out what it had been that woke her up. It sounded like John's voice, she thought, but then wondered if she'd dreamed it.

"Don't be crazy, Johnny," Kevin said as he stared at the gun. "That thing could go off in your hand."

"Or blow *your* head off!" Johnny reminded him.

"Ma?" Frank said as he walked into his guestroom to find her listening at her window to something outside. "What're you doin? I thought I heard somethin' in here. What is it?"

Suddenly, there was more yelling from up the street. At the same time, Lena and Frank realized it was Johnny's voice they heard. Without a word, Frank took off and ran outside. Lena was behind him as they ran over to Gina's house, where they saw all the lights on.

**

The wedding guests sweltered as they waited for "Ave Maria" to end so the wedding could start. Women and men alike fanned themselves and dabbed their brows with tissues. Finally, the music changed, and "Here Comes the Bride" bellowed from the church's organ pipes as the big arched double doors swung open wide. All the guests stood and turned to watch the beautiful bride come down the aisle to meet her groom as he anxiously waited for her. Johnny's palms were sweating, but it was because he was excited to see Rose in her gown walking toward him and into their future.

As he craned his neck to see his bride, Johnny noticed that Vinny did the same. Gina noticed, too, just like always. She looked down at her shoes, so she didn't have to watch Vinny long for Rose, the girl he'd never have for himself. Kevin watched Vinny, too. He knew Vinny had always wanted Rose for himself. But it infuriated Kevin that Vinny had stayed with Gina for so long when he really longed for Rose.

Rose briefly hesitated at the top of the aisle.

"Rosa?" Papa D said as he put his hand on her gloved one as she held his arm. But Rose didn't answer as she continued to walk down the aisle on her father's arm and the big doors closed behind her and the organ pipes played. Johnny's heart beat faster with each step Rose took toward him. He'd waited all his life for just this moment and just this woman. He knew their life would be incredible, and he felt blessed. It had been Rose's love, and the image of her face, that he'd held onto during the war. Rose was all he needed or wanted.

As they got to where Johnny stood, Rose looked at her handsome groom and met his gaze. For a split second the bride and groom connected more powerfully than ever, and both knew the future was theirs. But Rose couldn't get a breath of air, no matter how she tried. Her fingers tightened on Papa D's arm, the room seemed to sway, and her eyes rolled back.

"Rose? Rose!" Johnny yelled as he reached for her.

Her knees buckled, and Rose's body went limp as she collapsed in Johnny's arms. Gasps and screams bounced and echoed off the church walls as people clamored to see what had happened.

Moments later, a woman's voice wailed as she burst out the church doors and into the sunlight. "Morta! Morta! Morta!"

Oblivious to the pandemonium and hysterics, Johnny sat on the floor holding his unconscious bride as she took her last breath. "Rose! Wake up! Please. Please, Rose! Wake up! Oh God. Noooo!" he cried as he rocked her.

"Rosa! Dio mio! Mia Rosa!" Mama D screamed as she fell to her knees while Papa D held his heart. Gina fought the crowd to get to Celia, who stood frozen as she watched Rose.

"Celia!" Gina said as she grabbed her sister's hand. "C'mon! Come with me!" As Gina guided Celia out of the church, sirens filled the air as the fire brigade and an ambulance from St. Joseph's Hospital appeared. Uniformed attendants jumped out, hurriedly got a stretcher from the back of the ambulance, and rushed toward the church steps. But they couldn't get close to the church since the crowd had quickly tripled in size, with guests, passersby, and strangers all wanting to know what had happened at the usually quiet church in Inwood.

Police officers blew whistles, but the shrill sounds only added to the panicked chaos. "Make way! Step aside!" an officer yelled. "C'mon! Let these guys through!" Police officers swarmed the church grounds as they fought to control the crowds to make way for the ambulance workers.

By the time the men finally got to Rose, she was as white as her gown and soaked in sweat. Mama D wailed like a wounded wild animal. But no matter how loud she screamed, she couldn't release the guttural pain she'd bear for the next five decades. People tended to Papa D while an officer tried in vain to console Mama as three women fanned her with wedding programs. Johnny wouldn't let anyone touch Rose, but one ambulance worker managed to check for her pulse. He looked up and shook his head sadly at his partner and a nearby police officer.

*

"Woah. Johnny," Kevin said calmly as he put his hands up. "Let's talk. Just you and me."

"Talk?" Johnny said. "About what? How when you couldn't have her, you killed her?"

"Johnny, no. Not even close."

As he talked, Kevin kept his eyes on Johnny's hands. He deftly eased toward him while he kept Gina behind him. Johnny stepped back as Kevin got closer, a step at a time.

"You're full'a shit!" Johnny yelled as he waved the gun.

"No. That's not it. Let me talk to you, Johnny." The veteran cop stayed cool as he diverted Johnny and his gun away from Gina.

"You did it! You killed my Rose because you wanted her! You loved her, but she loved me!" Johnny yelled, as tears fell onto his red, wrinkled face.

"Kevin never wanted Rose," Gina tried to explain. "That was just Vinny causin' trouble, and I hated him for it!"

"Johnny, listen," Kevin said. "I love Gina. Always have."

"Dad! What are you doin'?" Frank yelled from behind Johnny. "Have you gone crazy? Put that gun down!"

"Get outta here, Frank! This ain't got nothin to do with you!"

"You kiddin'? I'm the one who stirred this up again. You wanna kill someone, this is on me."

"Good God, John!" Lena screamed as she ran closer.

"Have you lost your friggin' mind?"

Johnny waved the gun and pointed to where he wanted Kevin to move so he could turn and see Lena. But the sight of her only agitated him more, and his hand trembled as he pointed the gun at Kevin.

"She was murdered. Poisoned!" Johnny yelled. "And *this* piece of shit either did it because he wanted her and couldn't have her, or he knows who killed her and covered it up! Or was it that shit Vinny who did it? Did he take my Rose from me because he hated me that much? And maybe he made you cover it up for him because he had somethin' on you?"

Johnny took a menacing step toward Kevin as he waved the gun wildly. Kevin eyed the gun and tried to remain calm.

"Don't you dare!" Gina yelled as she stepped in front of Kevin and forcefully stared into Johnny's eyes.

"Gina, get inside the house," Kevin said in an even tone.

"Quit tryin' to protect him, Gina!" Johnny said. "He's a dirty cop! He did it or he's involved! Stop protectin' him!"

"You moron! Kevin's protectin' *me*!" Gina screamed.

Johnny's jaw dropped and he stepped back. "What?"

"Gina, go in the house. Now," Kevin repeated as he kept his hands up and his eyes on Johnny.

"It was *me*, Johnny," Gina said.

"What?" Johnny shook his head, more confused than ever. "*You*, Gina?"

"I mean, it was my *fault*!"

"What? Quit talkin' crazy—"

"Really. It was my fault, Johnny. I took my eyes off her. It was such a busy day. So much goin' on and all the excitement and chaos in the house. I took my eyes off her, just for a minute, and—"

"What the hell are you talkin' about?" Johnny tried to understand, but it made no sense.

"That day, everything was going wrong. One thing after the next. And Rose said somethin' about her nerves. I think she said her nerves were shot."

Gina dropped to her knees and sobbed. She couldn't go on. It hurt to even remember it all.

"What's that mean? *Her nerves were shot.* What the hell's that mean?" Johnny winced as he anxiously waved the gun.

"I guess Celia saw Rose's blue medicine bottle on her vanity table. She only wanted to help Rose. Celia poured *her* prescription medicine, her nerve medicine, from the brown bottle into Rose's stomach medicine in the blue bottle. Celia thought she was being nice by sharing her medicine and helping Rose to settle her nerves. She figured that since it helped her, her medication would fix Rose's nerves, too."

"Oh, God," Johnny whispered as his grip loosened on the gun. He took a step backward as if kicked in the gut and knocked off balance.

"No. Not Celia. God, no," Johnny shook his head, and he shut his eyes to block out the painful truth that had eluded him for decades.

"When she told me later that night, I made her swear not to ever tell another soul. Not ever. Can you imagine what they'd have thought back then? They might've thought Celia was dangerous to herself or others."

Gina cried harder and gulped and choked as she tried to go on. Johnny couldn't speak, couldn't think, and couldn't breathe.

"Johnny, I thought they'd take her from us and put her in one of those awful places! You know, an institution or an asylum! They used to warehouse people when they thought they might be dangerous, and I knew they'd never understand. Rose was already gone. I couldn't let them take Celia!"

"Not Celia," Johnny repeated in a barely audible whisper.

"Gina had asked me for help," Kevin added, "so I took the file. I did do that, Johnny. But it was to help, to protect *Celia*. You guys had lost your parents, your sister, and then Rose? That's more tragedy than one family can bear. Gina said that you and Celia were all she had left. You all had suffered so much, and all I wanted to do was help Gina. So I buried it. It seemed like the right thing to do back then. For all three of you."

"All these years?" Johnny suddenly erupted as he yelled at Gina. His face twisted and contorted in pained disbelief. "You been hidin' this from me for all these years?" Johnny turned toward Kevin. "And you! You *helped* her? You helped us? That was my Rose! My life! And she was carryin' . . . "

Johnny hung his head and sobbed huge, guttural sobs, unable to even say the words.

"Carryin'? Carryin' what, Johnny?" Gina asked.

Finally, Johnny summoned the courage to speak. The words were so painful he could barely form them in his mouth.

"Carryin' my baby!" he wailed.

"Oh, my God," Lena gasped as she covered her mouth in shock.

Gina's mouth dropped open wide as she absorbed the weight of what her brother had just disclosed. "She was pregnant?" Gina responded in disbelief. She turned to Kevin, "Did you know this?"

Kevin just hung his head in silence as realization quickly washed over Gina.

"Oh, Johnny. Oh, God," she whispered as she covered her mouth in utter shock.

"I had a right to know, Gina! A fuckin' right!" Johnny hollered as he again waved the gun wildly. "That was *my* fuckin' life, not yours! You don't get to decide how much I know about what happened to it and why it was robbed from me!"

"Dad! Enough! They were only tryin' to help. It's over now!" Frank yelled from behind him. "Let it go!"

But Johnny didn't think that was possible. "It'll never be over! You hear me? Never!" he yelled.

"It'll never be over because you're a coward, Dad!"

"What'd you call me?" Johnny challenged as he bowed up and tried to focus on his only son.

"You're a coward! You think you're a big, tough man—brave enough to dodge bullets and bombs on a battlefield—but you're too scared to simply show love to your own family!"

"That *was* my family that died in that church!" Johnny sobbed.

"*We're* your damn family! Frank shouted in disgust. "Don't you get it, old man? We're the ones who put up with your crap all these years. We're the ones who've loved you, been there for you, despite all your bullshit! But you're too damn busy living in the past to realize it! We're done living in the shadow of some ghost family that never even existed. We deserve better. Ma deserves better! She's loved you unconditionally, and you've never loved her back the way you should have. It takes courage to love, and sometimes, it hurts, but you've avoided it, at the expense of losing the only family you've ever had. So, yeah, I'd say you're a coward—and a goddamn fool!"

Johnny's eyes burned with searing fury as he lunged toward Frank to silence the words, which stung. All at once, Kevin and Frank dove on Johnny. They both fought to keep the gun in Johnny's hand pointed skyward.

CLICK! CLICK! CLICK!

As the men struggled to subdue Frank, the gun went off. Frank overpowered his dad and ripped the gun out of Johnny's trembling hand. Lena and Gina screamed, and so did the neighbors, from their porches, along with the few onlookers who'd dared to venture closer to the scene.

"It's okay, Dad!" Frank yelled. "It's okay!"

Some neighbors had run home when Frank and Kevin moved in on Johnny, afraid for their lives when the gun had fired. But Gina and Lena rushed toward Johnny, on the ground with Frank, as Kevin went for the gun. Instinctively, Kevin secured the scene.

"Firing pin failed," he said as he breathlessly examined the old Luger. "Shit, Johnny! What the hell?"

But Johnny didn't even see Kevin anymore, much less hear him as Frank held his sobbing dad on the ground.

"I can't lose you," Johnny cried. "Not you, too, Frank! I don't wanna lose you! God help me, I can't! I can't live through that!"

"Let's get 'im inside." Gina nodded toward her house. "We're givin' these people a show out here."

Lena could hardly speak as she clutched her chest, watching the most important people in her world be racked with pain, raw with years of grief and loss. She knelt beside Johnny where Frank held him and rocked him.

"We're here, Dad. We're not goin' anywhere. Ma and me, we're here for you. We'll always be here." Frank cradled his anguished father as Johnny wailed and cried out like an injured wild animal.

Lena knelt beside him and touched Johnny's arm. She'd always loved him, and she couldn't bear to see him in pain.

"We're goin' home. Right, John? We're goin' home. C'mon now."

Johnny wiped his eyes and looked at her. He reached for her as they both dissolved in tears, just as the blue flashing lights rolled up in front of Gina's home. A pair of uniformed cops got out, each with a hand on his sidearm, as they cautiously approached the scene.

Kevin discreetly slipped the Luger into his waistband in back as he walked toward the cops to do some damage control. No good would come of letting them haul Johnny off.

"How's it goin', guys?" he said as he shook the familiar officers' hands.

"Hey, Kevin. What's up, man? You got this, or what?"

"Yeah, yeah, yeah. Just a family thing. Disagreement, you know? But it's all good." Kevin exaggeratedly waved off the sobbing family behind him, as if the incident were no big deal, and he talked to the cops and steered them back to their patrol car.

"C'mon, John," Lena said. "Let's go home."

She and Frank helped Johnny to his feet. He was wobbly from the alcohol and weak from the past ten minutes, which had slammed into him like a runaway freight train. Frank steadied his dad as Lena wrapped an arm around John's waist for support.

"Jesus," Gina exclaimed. "What a night."

She and Frank watched as Lena and John slowly walked home, hand in hand, under the moonlight. It was a scene Frank had never witnessed as a boy.

Suddenly, Johnny stopped in his tracks as the realization of what just transpired hit him. He turned to face his wife as he gripped both her hands and tearfully confessed, "I love you, Lena. You asked if I loved you. I do. I *really* do love you."

Lena nodded. Tears filled her eyes as he gently cupped her face in both hands, leaned in, and kissed her ever so tenderly, as they both cried for all that was lost and all the years of heartache.

"Let's go home. I'll defrost some fagioli for you," Lena told John.

Johnny nodded, relieved and grateful for Lena. Maybe for the first time, he genuinely appreciated his wife.

"But first maybe you should take a shower. You smell like a distillery," Lena said. Hand in hand, they turned toward their house.

CHAPTER 20

Days later, and after his hangover wore off, Johnny planted pale-yellow hydrangeas outside their kitchen window. Lena handed him a glass of iced tea. "Oh, John! My favorites! I love that shade!"

Johnny took the tall glass with his gloved hand.

"I know—they're the color of your suit on our wedding day."

Lena's eyes teared as she sipped her tea. He remembered.

"I took Paul some tea down in the basement," Lena said as she struggled with the lump in her throat.

"That kid should be about done down there. It's been days," Johnny grumbled.

"John. Give the kid a break. He's givin' all the money from the sale of that stuff to the Autism Society."

"Yeah," Johnny nodded, missing his sweet sister. "Celia would like that. Yep, she's still helpin' people. That's Celia."

"Aye! Dad!" Frank yelled as he came up from the basement, pointing over his shoulder and rolling his eyes. "You better get down there. Paul's found that old violin and is going berserk."

"Go." Lena laughed as she turned back toward the door.

Johnny followed Frank down the steps and into the basement. "Eh, you're not still gripin' now, I see. Hard work pays off, right?" Johnny called out to his grandson.

"Grandpa! Look at this! Oh, wow! This is a find, a major find!" Paul excitedly said, as he held up the old violin in its original case.

"I'd hoped you'd sweat a little more while you paid your penance for that academic probation," Johnny grumbled. "You kids got it too easy today."

"Are you kiddin' me? Just seeing this was worth it!" Paul proclaimed.

Frank and Johnny both rolled their eyes.

"Not the academic probation." Paul laughed. "I mean, cleanin' the basement out for days was worth the work just to see this masterpiece and hold it. Wait'll I tell you about this, its history, who's played it. No one's gonna believe this! Just wait till I tell you about it!"

"I know all about that violin." Johnny laughed. "It was given to me a long, long time ago by your grandpa, your mom's father. Been down here in this basement locked away with lots'a old stuff from a long time ago."

"Your mom knows the history of it," Frank told Paul. "She can tell you all about that thing."

"This *thing* is a Stradivarius," Paul corrected. "The guys in the band would freak if they saw this! Filippo Filicchi brought it to the United States way back. I've read about him and his work. This is amazing, Pop! And it's in my grandparents' basement? Are you friggin' kidding me?"

"Supposedly your mom's family was said to have something to do with how that violin came to be. I can't recall the whole story, but her parents always said there was some connection to the family, but you'd have to ask your mom about it. I do remember, though, that there was some confusion about the spelling of Filicchi and how the name got mangled when the family came over from Italy."

"I can't believe this!" Paul gushed as he gingerly held the violin. "This is a piece of musical history right here! I learned all about it in music theory class, and now I'm holding the actual instrument in my hands. This is crazy!"

Frank and Johnny shot each other a look again. It was at that moment they knew Paul should follow his passions, music, or whatever made him *that* excited and happy.

"See there?" Johnny grabbed Paul's neck from the back and gently squeezed as they started walking slowly. "There's a payoff for workin' hard. You should listen to your grandpa,

Paul. Each generation, we listen to the previous one so we can keep the good stuff goin'. It's been like that forever. Family, history, and the stories gotta be preserved and handed down. It's important to know about the old days. I've got some stories you should hear sometime. Let's plan to talk more. It'll be important to you and to your kids one day."

Frank watched his dad and his son from the back, thankful and relieved. When they got to the stairs that led up to the kitchen, Johnny stopped and called over his shoulder, "Frank. We're makin' some lunch. You want me to make you a sandwich?"

"Sure, Dad. That'd be nice. Thanks."

Frank smiled as he grabbed a broom.

"I'll be up in a few. Just gonna sweep up the last of it back here."

He quickly swept the concrete floor, creating dust that danced in the light beam from the workshop's door that was ajar. Frank stopped sweeping and hesitantly approached the door and pushed it open fully. He gasped as he looked at the small, empty room.

"Rest in peace, Rose," he said as he backed out of the room and switched off the light. But his eyes spotted something near his shoe. He bent down and picked it up.

Frank leaned the broom against the wall by the steps and ran upstairs. As he opened the door to step into the kitchen, Johnny handed Paul a wad of cash. "Hey! Dad! What're you doin' payin' him when he's screwin' off at school? This was punishment to clean your basement!"

"I'm not *payin'* Paul for cleanin' my basement! I'm payin' him to fix my friggin' yard out there after all this time!" Johnny exaggeratedly yelled. "Whadda we live like animals? I work hard. I wanna come home to a nice house with a nice lawn. The jackass that tore up my grass must'a had shitty parenting to leave it like that all this time. But now, Paul here, who was raised right, will go and fix it."

Frank appreciated his dad's attempt at complimenting his parenting of Paul. It was Johnny's style. Frank sat down at his usual seat at the kitchen table and looked down at the diagonally cut sandwich on his plate. He picked up a half, turned it over, and smiled.

"Nope. I'm pretty sure that jackass had great parents, too," he said as he took a bite. "The best, I'd say."

When Johnny sat down at the head of the table, there was a small, dark lock of hair, tied in a thin pink satin ribbon, beside his plate. He jumped a little at the sight of it, then looked over at Frank, who winked. Johnny silently slipped the lock into his pocket.

"Paul, you need'a make sure you call and have that dumpster picked up now that it's full. Don't wait. I don't want all that junk out there all week, clutterin' up my driveway," Johnny grumbled.

"I know," Paul said, as he rolled his eyes and sighed.

"Somebody's comin' tomorrow to pick up all the good stuff. I told 'em to make the check out directly to the autism group.

Lena and Johnny looked at each other, and she reached out and touched his arm. "I miss her, too. Celia is still sweet Celia. Just who she was meant to be, just who she'll always be."

"Forever," Johnny added as he chewed.

Frank watched his parents. He was happy for them, but disappointment soon washed over him as it became clear that he'd blown it with Debbie. That ship had sailed.

*

Days later, but not until he'd watched the dumpster removal guys to make sure they didn't tear up his lawn, Johnny went for a drive. This time, he took their Buick. But like always, he drove with the window down and the wind blowing his hair. As he passed Willow Tavern, he thought he saw Kevin's car in the parking lot. Johnny turned around and went back to check.

"Hey. Buy you a drink?" he said as he sat down next to Kevin at the bar. "I think I owe you one."

"Make it a bottle, then." Kevin laughed as he shook Johnny's hand.

After a little while, the men talked and relaxed, glad the truth was finally out.

"Hey, I gotta run," Johnny said. "I've got somethin' I need to do. But if you're free, why don't you meet us here next

Saturday night. There's a show."

"Yeah. All right. Sounds good."

Johnny smacked Kevin on the back as he left.

Forty minutes later, Johnny sat alone on a bench in Atlantic Beach overlooking the ocean. He leaned back and inhaled the salty air as breezes blew and seagulls chattered. He recalled the scent of Rose's perfume mixed with the salty air. He reached into his pocket and pulled out the lock of hair he had enshrined in his basement footlocker for over half a century. He slipped the ribbon off the strands, closed his eyes, and gently kissed the hair before he held it into the wind and watched the strands blow lazily away, as he whispered to himself, "Our forever starts now. You *are* eternally *my* Rose."

EPILOGUE

On Saturday, Johnny held Lena's hand as they walked into Willow Tavern. Frank had already found them a good table right in front of the band that had just started playing. Just as Johnny sat down, Kevin and Gina arrived.

Sharon, the cocktail waitress, took Gina's order as Johnny leaned toward Kevin and said, "Can you believe that's my grandson up there playin' keyboard? He's incredible! And look how happy he is doin' what he loves!"

Frank gave Sharon his order and noticed Debbie in a booth with a girlfriend. Their eyes locked, just for a moment, and Frank raised his glass to her and smiled.

"What can I do for you, Frank?" Sharon smiled, her breasts eye level and awkwardly close to him, as usual.

*

Johnny spent the next months trying to digest the news that it had been Celia, sweet, innocent Celia, who'd only tried to help Rose and instead created a deadly poison by mixing medications. Celia had died without ever knowing her actions had led to the death of her beloved Rose.

"I still can't believe it," Lena said. "The simplest, most

well-intended thing, and look. And who would have thought when I heard that woman yell, 'Morta! Morta! Morta!' and I called for help by knocking on that door, that I'd be standin' here today *with you*. I knew you were gettin' married that weekend, of course, but there were six weddings scheduled that day, and I had no idea that it was your wedding happening at the time."

"I guess we're right where we're meant to be in time and space, but it's crazy. You know how Celia always liked to help people and make 'em feel better?" John said. "It's who she *was*."

"It's who she'll always be," Lena corrected. "Like you've heard me say before, we are who we are. You know? And who we make ourselves to be is the last picture people will have of us. That's why every day's important, John."

Lena nodded as she blew on a spoonful of marinara to cool it. Then, without a word, she held the spoon so John could taste it. He kissed his fingers dramatically, and then leaned down and gently kissed Lena on the cheek. She turned. Their eyes locked. The spoon hit the floor just as John scooped her in his arms and kissed her fully and urgently, as if to make up for lost time. Lena shut her eyes and melted into him. She saw the young, handsome soldier whose love she'd always wanted. Johnny lifted Lena onto the counter, seeing her for the first time, while feeling he'd loved her for decades.

Thirty minutes later, the unattended saucepot violently rattled as marinara bubbled down the stove front and onto the floor. It was unlike Lena to leave her sauce unattended.

"What the," Frank said as he came in the back door and instantly ran, stepping in tomato sauce, to turn off the smoking pot.

He looked in the living room, and then in the den, and realized that no one was home. He presumed his parents had gone out and that his mom had forgotten to turn off the stove.

"Seriously?" he mumbled to himself. "Those two are gettin' too old to live alone! They're gonna burn the whole house down!"

Since the house was empty and the sauce was obviously ruined, he knew he wouldn't find dinner there. Frank turned off the kitchen lights and then went home to scrounge something for dinner.

A little while later Johnny and Lena came downstairs wearing only white bathrobes and smiles. Johnny flipped on the kitchen light.

"Oh, God!" Lena exclaimed. "She's *still* sayin' it! I still got it!" joked Johnny, laughing for the first time he could remember.

"I like that," Lena smiled.

"I know. I could tell."

"No. Hearin' you laugh. I like hearin' you laugh, John."

"And I liked that, too, as I'm sure you could also tell." Johnny grinned, deepening the dimple in his chin that Lena had loved for years.

Lena laughed. But he touched her arm and said, "No, lemme be serious. I love makin' you smile. You deserve to smile and to be happy, Lena."

He leaned down and kissed her, then suddenly pulled away and added, "Well, okay. And that. Since we agreed on our kid, we'd have clarity and open communication, I'm clearly statin' that I like both those things, and that I love you, Mrs. Mastantuono."

P.S.

ACKNOWLEDGMENTS

The author would like to acknowledge the contributions of
the following individuals who have invested their time,
talents, and feedback in support of this book:

My son, Louis Mastantuono.
Through thick and thin–because you're what life's all about.

My grandson, John Michael Mastantuono.
No matter where, or how far, always know John you're with
me.

Mary E. Davis, for sharing your talents and enthusiasm in
telling my story.

Scott Pardo, for taking this journey with me through all the
highs and lows, in business and in friendship. Thank you.

My dear friends,

Lucy and Ralph Palleschi
Vincent and Marie Vicareo
Alfred Lagonegro
Nick Christophers
Felice Harwood
Michael Dudek
Cindy Alzado
Mike Heller
Joel Getreu
Helaina Gillette
Don Henderson
Fred Messinetti

With love and gratitude for your friendship and steadfast
support, thank you!

Our wonderful readers:

Jillian Rivera, Beatrice McGee, David Echeverria, John Anthony, Amanda Pearson, Katrina Nancy Robin, Allison C. Mel, Donna Van-Cott Healy, Sharyn Loshin O'Mara, Leslie Ogden, Andria Greeney and Rina Marie.

Thank you all for the gift of your time and invaluable feedback.

And a very special thanks of appreciation to my dear friend and colleague Augustine "Augie" Covert, for all of his inspiration, input, and countless hours assisting in bringing this long-awaited endeavor to life.

IN MEMORIAM

JOHN FRANK MASTANTUONO
My father who loved me unconditionally and instilled in
me to never give up on my dreams in life.
He will always be my hero.

ANGELA ROSE DEFABRIZIO
The woman I never knew, but who played a major role in
my family's story. Rest in eternal peace.

ANTOINETTE "MAMA" DEFABRIZIO
Mother to Rose, who was always so loving to me, my
mother, and of course my father. honored and grateful that
she shared all of her most painful and precious memories
with me.

ALLISON MARGOLIES
My guardian angel. Thank you for always believing in me. In
my thoughts all the time.

DR. JOHN VALENTINO
My dearly departed "brother from another mother". You're
sorely missed.

MIKE "BOSSA" NOVA
No matter where life will lead me, you will always be with me
in spirit for the rest of my journey.

NEWS ARTICLES

LIFE Magazine

THIS IS THE HOUSE THE COUPLE HAD BOUGHT WHEN HE RETURNED FORM THE ARMY   AFTER BURIAL WEDDING CEREMONY ROSE PINNED A CORSAGE ON HER MOTHER

A BRIDE DIES AT HER WEDDING

THEY POSED TOGETHER WHILE HE WAS IN UNIFORM

Rose De Falco and John Mennato are close, they were high-school students in Central, Long Island. They were very sweethearts but she was passed the five-year could get married. John went into the Army for two and a half years. And once he got he was released and they decided to get married. Rose felt like a fairytale bride. Both her and their final preparations carefully, John already a good job.

He even found a house and with his mother's help bought it. Then they set the date, the first real item the flurry of last-minute plans. Rose bought a wedding dress. John bought a ring and booked a car for their honeymoon in Atlantic City. Then hired a photographer to take pictures of the wedding. On the morning of the wedding, even things he knew it was supposed to bring. Led back, John

ON HER FATHER'S ARM ROSE STARTS UP THE STEPS TO THE CHURCH. "I CARE FOR MY ARM, MY BEAUTIFUL LITTLE GIRL," HE SAID. THE TWO PRACTICED THIS

LIFE Magazine

A LONG ISLAND GIRL WHO WAITED ALL THROUGH THE WAR TO MARRY
HER HIGH-SCHOOL SWEETHEART FALLS DEAD AT THE CHURCH DOOR

New York Daily News

DAILY NEWS, MONDAY, OCTOBER 7, 1946

Happily bride-to-be Rose De Fabriis dabs on last bit of makeup before ceremony.

Bride, 21, Falls Dead Walking Up Altar Aisle

By HENRY LEE

Yesterday was the day that pretty Rose De Fabriis, 21, was going to trounce all her ills. After almost three years of worry while her childhood sweetheart served in the Army, after months and months of eager, happy buying and planning and outfitting a home, yesterday was her day of days— her wedding day.

As her father, Louis De Fabriis, proudly stands by. Rose plan a corsage on her mother's arm. Healthy and vigorous, Rose quit her job eight months ago to prep for her marriage.

Surrounded by attendants, Rose is few minutes from marrying—and death.

300 Join Hunt For Boy, Lost In N. J. Swamp

By William Price and Jamie Desmond

The Voice Sings Blues Off Key as He Quits Wife

Hollywood, Oct. 6 (P)—Singer Frankie Sinatra, whose crooning has made weak thousands of bobby socks to the verge of hysteria, has separated from his sometime wife, Nancy, he announced today.

New York Daily News

DAILY NEWS, FRIDAY, OCTOBER

'A THING WHICH MAKES MEN WEEP'

Leaving St. Joachim's Church after funeral service are Louis De Fabrizio, father of dead girl (supported by friends), Johnny Mastantuono, bridegroom-to-be (light coat) and Mrs. De Fabrizio, the girl's mother (assisted by Johnny).

Death Bride Is Buried at Tearful Rite

By ART SMITH

The bells of St. Joachim's in Cedarhurst, L. I., tolled a carillon of grief yesterday as Johnny Mastantuono buried his childhood sweetheart, Angela Rose De Fabrizio, the 21-year-old girl who fell dead last Sunday as she walked down the aisle to become his wife.

The funeral was held in St. Joachim's rather than in Our Lady of Good Counsel, at Inwood, L. I.,

(NEWS foto by Edger)
On Sunday they were ready to serve as ushers at the wedding of Angela Rose De Fabrizio—now they bear her casket.

AUTHOR'S NOTE

Valued Reader,

I would like to extend my gratitude to you for taking the time to read "Eternally Rose". I realize there are many great authors and an abundance of truly wonderful stories available for you to choose from. I'm humbled and grateful that you've chosen to invest your valuable time reading my story. Thank you!

If you would like to share your thoughts on the book, or just say hi, I welcome the opportunity to connect with you and invite you to reach out to me—via my website or social media.

With my sincere appreciation,

Lou "Frank" Mastantuono

THE AUTHOR

LOU MASTANTUONO (pka Lou Mast) is a show business veteran, having produced and developed various projects for stage, screen and radio in a career spanning over forty years.

Some of his notable projects include bringing the highly acclaimed Off-Broadway production *Squonk* to the Helen Hayes Theater in NYC, and penning the Billboard Number One Dance Chart hit *Bring Your Love Back* (1985).

As an actor, some of his credits include *The Legend of Billy Jack*, *Amongst Friends*, *Prizzi's Honor*, as well as various roles in short films, television pilots and documentaries.

Eternally Rose is Lou's life-long passion project launched on a promise made to his mother, in her final hours, while battling lung cancer.

 eternallyrosebook.com

@eternallyrosebook

@lmastsr

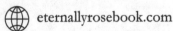

CPSIA information can be obtained
at www.ICGtesting.com
Printed in the USA
BVHW071206110822
644347BV00014B/1005